Photo by Rey Pamatmat

Jeff Barry as Caliban in the Yale School of Drama
production of *Rough Magic*.

ROUGH MAGIC

BY
ROBERTO AGUIRRE-SACASA

★

★

DRAMATISTS
PLAY SERVICE
INC.

ROUGH MAGIC received its world premiere at the Yale School of Drama (James Bundy, Dean; Mark Bly, Chair of Playwriting), in New Haven, Connecticut, opening on April 24, 2003. It was directed by David Muse; the set design was by Blythe R. D. Quinlan; the costume design was by Jessica Ford; the lighting design was by Scott Bolman; the sound design was by Daniel Baker; the video design was by Daniel Baker, Taylor Krauss, and Blythe R. D. Quinlan; the choreography was by Wade Laboissonniere; the fight choreography was by Rick Sordelet; the dramaturgy was by Emily V. Shooltz; and the production stage manager was Molly McCarter. The cast was as follows:

LINDA SUMMERS/ALECTO .... Heather Mazur
PROSPERO .... James Lloyd Reynolds
MIRANDA .... Mikelle Johnson
MELANIE PORTER .... Tijuana T. Ricks
CHET BAXTER .... Greg Felden
ARIEL .... Jacob Knoll
SASIA .... Christianna Nelson
CALIBAN .... Jeff Barry
SHYLOCK .... Anthony Manna
CAIUS MARCIUS .... Adam Saunders
TISIPHONE .... David Bardeen
MEGAERA/DR. ROSEMARY RIDGEON .... Anita Gandhi

ROUGH MAGIC received its regional premiere at the Hangar Theatre (Kevin Moriarty, Artistic Director; Lisa Bushlow, Executive Director), in Ithaca, New York, opening on July 29, 2005. It was directed by Kevin Moriarty; the set design was by Wilson Chin; the costume design was by Greg Robbins; the lighting design was by Deborah Constantine; the sound design and original music were by Sarah Pickett; the fight choreography was by Norm Johnson; the casting was by Stephanie Klapper; and the stage manager was Melissa Daroff. The cast was as follows:

LINDA SUMMERS	Sarah K. Chalmers
PROSPERO	William Parry
MIRANDA	Amanda Sox
MELANIE PORTER	Heather Mazur
CHET BAXTER	Greg Felden
ARIEL	Russ Salmon
SASIA	Jillian Fratkin
CALIBAN	Matthew Montelongo
SHYLOCK	David Romm
CAIUS MARCIUS	Jade Rothman
TISIPHONE	John Misselwitz
MEGAERA	Joshua Williams
ALECTO	Christopher Hollowell
DR. ROSEMARY RIDGEON	Camilla Schade

CHARACTERS
(in speaking order)

LINDA SUMMERS, a graduate student at Columbia University

PROSPERO, a sorcerer

MIRANDA, his daughter

MELANIE PORTER, a pretty dramaturg, raven-haired, wears glasses, thirty

CHESTER "CHET" BAXTER, a cute lifeguard, seventeen-ish

ARIEL, Prospero's son, an enslaved spirit, blue-eyed

SASIA, his twin sister, also enslaved, also blue-eyed

TRACY, Melanie's sister, heard only on speakerphone

CALIBAN, Prospero's first-born, escaped from Prospero's island

SHYLOCK, owner of the Alabaster bookstore on Twelfth Street

CAIUS MARCIUS, a Roman General

TISIPHONE, a fabulous drag performer, the first Fury

MEGAERA, one of Tisiphone's back-up singers, also a Fury

ALECTO, Tisiphone's second back-up singer, the last Fury

DR. ROSEMARY RIDGEON, a doctor at Bellevue Psychiatric Hospital, British

PLACE

Prospero's island, the island of Manhattan. Various locations.

TIME

The present, one long night during a terrible heatwave.

NOTE: The play should take place on a Shakespearean stage, mostly bare. The characters always tell us where they are, so each location can be suggested with the absolute minimum amount of stuff. Maybe a book motif dominates. Or a map.

This play should fly like the wind.

Doubling is okay. One actor can play Tracy, Megaera, and Dr. Rosemary Ridgeon. Another actor can play both Linda Summers and Alecto.

ROUGH MAGIC

ACT ONE

Before the play begins, audience members see a projection of Henry Fuseli's famous painting The Tempest, *showing Miranda, Prospero, Ariel, and Caliban. Prospero holds an enormous book in his arms.*

The lights shift, the Fuseli painting disappears, and we are in a classroom at Columbia University. Graduate student Linda Summers is in mid-lecture. Her hair is pulled back in a bun, her lipstick is red, and her glasses are foxy.

LINDA. The subject is magic: What is it? Does it exist? And, if so, *where* does it exist?
  In a handful of sand?
  In the petals of a flower?
  In a shard of ancient stone?
(Beat. Smiles.) I apologize for our — accommodations. Columbia University values the Study of Magic enough to offer a course in it — during summer session, granted, taught by a graduate student — but not enough to give us a room with windows or a working air conditioner. Not even during this, the worst heat wave in New York City's history. *(Beat.)* But let's not dwell, let's dive in. *(Checks her notes.)* We're starting today with the most powerful magician who ever lived, an Italian sorcerer who amassed all the secrets of magic from creation to destruction to re-creation into one volume — and can anyone name him? *(No answer.)* I'll give you a hint, people: Shakespeare wrote a play about him. *(Still no answer.)* Prospero, people, from *The Tempest*, although Shakespeare's Prospero is very, *very* different from the real Prospero, the *real, liv-*

ing, breathing Prospero, who was Genoa's Duke (not Milan's) from — when, people? (It was in your reading last night.) *(Nothing.)* From 1498–1566, when three merchant ships he'd sent to Cathay, to China, returned carrying a disease-ridden crew infected with — can anyone guess? *(Silence.)* The Black Death, people, which killed over half of Genoa's population.

The surviving half blamed Prospero for the plague and exiled him. Put him on a captainless ship, him and a thousand stinking, diseased corpses, bound for doom, and — what happened, people, does anyone know?

Is Prospero dead? *Did* he drown when that rotten carcass of a ship broke apart? Hmm? (Possibly, though magicians are notoriously hard to kill.) Or is he out there somewhere? Working on his book, burning with hatred for Genoa, the city that betrayed him, plotting his revenge, perfecting his magic? *(Short pause.)* I like to think so. That he's alive still, perhaps — as Shakespeare's play suggests — on an enchanted island, somewhere in the Mediterranean ... *(Thunderclap. Lightning, sounds of a hurricane. Linda is gone. Prospero, black-robed, white-bearded, carrying a staff in one hand and manacles in the other, rages in with the storm, bellowing:)*

PROSPERO. WIND — WAVES — THUNDER — LIGHT-NING! *(A young girl, Miranda, runs onstage after him. She's terrified. She yells to be heard over the storm's roaring.)*

MIRANDA. Father — can't you see? There's a ship — please — they'll all drown!

PROSPERO. Let them! Let the ocean be their grave! *(A terrific thunderclap.)*

MIRANDA. PLEASE — the people! *(Another one.)* Why are you doing this?

PROSPERO. Your brother has escaped! With my book — my Art! *(He throws the chains and manacles at her.)*

MIRANDA. What? *(Prospero lunges at her, grabs her by the shoulders, and pulls her in close.)*

PROSPERO. Your monstrous, misshapen, *malignant* brother — has stolen my Art and even now kicks his way towards freedom! *(Turns back to the raging sea.)* So let the waves crush him! Let the tides pull him under! And once he's drowned, once his lungs are choked with salt water, then will I calm the storm and beg the ocean deliver his body to me, cradled in a hand of foam!

MIRANDA. But the ship — you'll dash it to pieces — the people!

8

PROSPERO. LET — THEM — PERISH! *(The loudest thunder-clap of them all. The terrifying sound of a ship breaking apart as the lights crossfade to another part of the stage: a sidewalk café in New York City. Snappy, fun music — like the theme from* Sex and the City *— starts to play. Chet, a cute lifeguard, sits at a table. He's wearing flip-flops, baggy swim trunks, and his funky Hawaiian shirt is open, revealing his tanned, cut chest. Next to him is an orange life-saving device. Melanie, very pretty, enters and approaches Chet. She wears glasses.)*

MELANIE. Chester?

CHET. Melanie?

MELANIE. Hi. Chester Baxter?

CHET. Yeah. Well, Chet. Hi.

MELANIE. Hi, it's nice to meet you finally, I've heard so much about you from my sister.

CHET. Yeah, me, too. *(Beat.)* Uhm, is this okay? Sitting outside? I know the heat and all —

MELANIE. No, no, this is fine. *(Melanie sits at the café table. Smiles uncomfortably. Chet holds out a drink to her.)*

CHET. I ordered us frozen margaritas. Because of the heat? And Tracy said you liked margaritas?

MELANIE. I do, thanks. Sorry I'm late, by the way.

CHET. It's no problem. Were you working?

MELANIE. At Morgan Stanley, yes. I've been temping there for … ten years, on and off. Since I was twenty. *(Beat.)* It's like committing suicide very, very slowly.

CHET. Well, sure, especially compared to — I mean, you work in the theatre, right? Tracy said you're, like, a director?

MELANIE. I'm a dramaturg. *(Melanie sneezes.)*

CHET. Gesundheit. What's a dramaturg do?

MELANIE. Well … it depends. I work closely with the director and the playwright, I do research, I help with revisions — script revisions — I suggest cuts. I tell the director what I see in rehearsal, blocking and, you know: "Does this serve the text?" *(Embarrassed.)* It's hard to explain in the — the abstract. Much more so than what you do, which is … *(Melanie is eyeing Chet's life-preserver with some skepticism.)* Tracy mentioned that you're a — um — a lifeguard …

CHET. Yeah, at Coney Island. You know, in Brooklyn? *(Short, weird pause.)*

MELANIE. And lifeguarding, that's a — that's a full-time thing?

CHET. During summer — full-time. During the school year —

9

just weekends at the Y. The YMCA? I'm off today because the pool's closed because of the water shortage. *(Beat.)* But, I mean, if someone's drowning, even if I'm off-duty, I'm gonna save them.

MELANIE. Oh, well, sure. *(Beat.)* And, ahh, how does that work when you're — uhm — *not* near a body of water?

CHET. We don't *just* save people from drowning.

MELANIE. Well, of course not. *(Melanie sneezes.)*

CHET. Gesundheit. *(Holds out a napkin for her.)* Here.

MELANIE. Thanks. *(She takes it.)* I'm just getting over a summer cold. It's been dreadful.

CHET. Yeah. Although, with all the vitamin D I absorb from the sun, I never get sick. *(Melanie is unsure how to respond.)* Oh, don't worry, I know all the risks — skin cancer, chlorine poisoning, shark attacks — but I'm genetically pre-disposed to being a lifeguard. It's in my heritage. My dad was a lifeguard — *(Showing her.)* Here, check it out, this was his whistle — my granddad was a lifeguard, going way back. For, like, generations. Which is weird because we're originally from Scotland, my family is, although not really *that* weird 'cause my ancestors were highlanders. You know, like Rob Roy? In battle, the highlanders didn't fear death. In fact, they welcomed it, because they knew that when they died, all their friends, all their family that had died in battle before them, would be there, waiting for them with their swords raised. *(Beat.)* And, like, being a lifeguard continues that.

MELANIE. I — I never thought of life-guarding as the kind of … profession that gets passed down from generation to generation.

CHET. *(Proudly.)* I can hold my breath for three minutes, twenty-nine seconds. *(Melanie is looking at her watch.)*

MELANIE. Fascinating …

CHET. Hey, can I be, uhm, forward with you?

MELANIE. Uh …

CHET. I know we just met and all, but I was wondering? If you're not doing anything this Saturday night? If you would maybe consider being my date for the prom?

MELANIE. Oh, I don't know, Chet, I'm not much of a — *(Beat.)* Wait. When you say "prom," what do you mean exactly? Do you mean — ?

CHET. The senior prom. *(Short pause.)*

MELANIE. How *old* are you, Chet?

CHET. Me? I'm eighteen. *(All in a huff, Melanie stands, takes money out of her purse.)* What's wrong?

MELANIE. You're *eighteen?*

CHET. In two weeks.

MELANIE. *(Mortified.)* (Oh my God …)

CHET. Give me a chance —

MELANIE. Look, Chet, you're cute, *and* you're — *(Mini-beat.)* roguish, *and* you save lives, but there are limits. Not at your age, for the rest of us, I mean. *(Chet stands.)* Please, don't let's have a scene. I think you're very nice, I do, and I like this café, so I'm not gonna tell the waiter he's been serving alcohol to a *minor,* but — *(Game over.)* Goodbye, Chet Baxter. Call me. Once you've — pushed through puberty.

CHET. Wait, before you go —

MELANIE. I've already left. You don't see me. *(She starts striding away, but —)*

CHET. I know about your magic. *(Melanie stops, turns back.)*

MELANIE. My what?

CHET. Tracy and I were talking and she was telling me about how you have these, like, magical powers. *(Short pause. Then:)*

MELANIE. My sister has no idea what she's talking about. *(She starts to go again.)*

CHET. She said that's how come you have a lot of problems — you know, like, "issues" — connecting with people and letting your defenses down. *(Beat.)* We can talk about it if you want. I mean, I like to think of myself as being a pretty open person.

MELANIE. I don't do it anymore, Chet, I don't even talk about it. *(Beat.)* Tracy shouldn't have told you.

CHET. She didn't say much. I mean, except that you could, uhm — *(Chet quickly looks into the palm of his hand, where he's clearly made notes for his date.)* "unlock characters from dramatic texts, from any dramatic play."

MELANIE. Not any, no. *(Surprising even herself, Melanie continues.)* Shakespeare worked best, and the Greeks, and musicals, and some-times Tennessee Williams (I don't know why). Sometimes I *could* set characters free, sometimes I couldn't. Sometimes, if they were clever enough — or desperate enough — they escaped on their own. They always caused trouble. I gave it up years ago.

CHET. How come, did something bad happen? *(Pause.)*

MELANIE. Uhm. Once, when I was in high school — *like you are now* — I tried to set Romeo free. I wanted him to be my date for Homecoming, but Tybalt got out instead. He … started a fight —

sliced the Homecoming King's ear off — almost got me expelled ...

CHET. And, wait, that's why you gave it up? *(Beat.)* Because that kind of thing happens at my school, like, every day.

MELANIE. Maybe to you, Chet.

CHET. I think magic's totally cool.

MELANIE. It's totally not. *(Mini-pause.)* End of story. And — end of date. Goodbye, Chet. *Really* this time. *(Melanie leaves, sneezing. Chet remains behind, perplexed — but glowing a bit. The lights shift. Chet exits and a spot slowly comes up on Prospero. It is like the sun burning through clouds. He is on a beach, littered with drowned corpses, picking through the bodies with his daughter Miranda. She is carrying a small, limp body in her arms. She holds it up for Prospero to see.)*

MIRANDA. Look at this one, Father. He's just a little boy, and you've killed him! *(She looks around at all the carnage.)* You've killed them all! *(Prospero tosses aside another corpse like it's a rag doll.)*

PROSPERO. And none of them Caliban! Your brutish brother has slipped through my fingers like an eel.

MIRANDA. I'm glad! At least one of us has escaped you! *(Miranda gasps at her own audacity. She looks panicked. Prospero strides to her, stops, smiles, and strikes her across the face.)*

PROSPERO. Insolent! *(He turns from her, calls out:)* Sasia! Ariel! *(Two beautiful creatures enter, a brother and sister. They are blue-eyed — and deadly.)*

SASIA and ARIEL. *(In unison.)* Yes, Father.

PROSPERO. Caliban has fled our island with my book of spells, my Art. He has somehow loosed his chains — *(He looks at Miranda suspiciously.)* and vanished. Find him. Return him — and my book — to me — and you shall be as free as mountain winds.

SASIA and ARIEL. *(In unison.)* Yes, Father.

PROSPERO. Fail me — or try to escape yourselves — and I will find the strongest oak tree growing and bind you into its knotty entrails for twelve winters.

SASIA and ARIEL. *(In unison.)* Yes, Father.

PROSPERO. Pressed in the pages of my Art there is a flower that blooms lily-white, but turns dark violet when plucked. *(Prospero produces a flower from the sleeves of his robe.)* Here is its twin. Take this bloom. Use it. It will lead you to its mate like a beacon. *(Ariel takes the flower.)*

ARIEL. Thank you, Father.

PROSPERO. You will be under my protection. Nothing will be

able to harm you.

ARIEL and SASIA. Thank you, Father.

PROSPERO. Sasia.

SASIA. Father? *(Prospero takes a sheet of parchment from the sleeve of his robe.)*

PROSPERO. To help you, I give you the gift of fire. *(Sasia takes the sheet.)*

SASIA. Thank you, Father. *(Prospero produces another sheet of parchment from the sleeve of his robe.)*

PROSPERO. Ariel. *(Ariel takes the sheet.)* I give you —'invisibility.

ARIEL. Thank you, Father.

PROSPERO. To both of you — *(He raises his arms.)* Transport across the ocean! *(A flash of light. Prospero, Miranda, Ariel, and Sasia are gone. The sound of a telephone ringing. The lights rise on Melanie's book-lined apartment, just as she's coming home, closing the door behind her. She sneezes —)*

MELANIE. God bless me. *(Answers the telephone. It's a cordless, so Melanie can walk around her apartment doing apartment stuff.)* Hello? ... Tracy, hi, yeah, I just got home. ... Yes, I met him at — Probably not ... Order of importance or alphabetically? ... Number One, he's a lifeguard ... Right — yes — at Coney Island. ... Which makes him — Which means he's — No, a *carny*, I was gonna say ... And Number Two, how dare you — how *dare* you — tell him about my magic? You're my sister, Tracy! You of all people should know that we can't run around telling *everyone* about — *(Melanie drops the mail she was going through.)* Hang on, Tracy, I'm gonna put you on hands-free, I have to — *(Melanie puts the phone on speaker.)*

TRACY'S VOICE. — Don't you put me on speaker, Mel, I can't hear a *flipping* thing when I'm on — *(Beat.)* You put me on speaker, didn't you? This is me on speaker, isn't it?

MELANIE. Hang up if you want.

TRACY'S VOICE. I told Chet about your magic because it's time you started *dealing!* Whatever happened — that was years ago!

MELANIE. Okay, we're not having this conversation again.

TRACY'S VOICE. Give yourself a break. Chet's a nice guy. He's sweet, he's adorable, he tans evenly. *(During the above, Melanie has been looking at her floor concernedly. She bends down, touches it, brings her hand back up to her face.)*

MELANIE. Uh, Tracy? There are all these footprints, wet foot-prints, leading from the fire escape to my bedroom. I think — I

think someone's in the apartment with me … *(Short pause. Then:)*
TRACY'S VOICE. OHMYGODMELANIEGETOUTNOW!!!
MELANIE. SHHHHH! Lower your voice …
TRACY'S VOICE. LOWER MY VOICE?! Excuse me, isn't this New York City? Aren't you a single woman living alone in New York City? GET — OUT — NOW!
MELANIE. Number One: Thanks for reminding me I'm single. Number Two: Shhh, I'm gonna try to surprise him —
TRACY'S VOICE. I'm calling the police!
MELANIE. Can you wait one second, please?
TRACY'S VOICE. I'm calling Chet!
MELANIE. What? Why?
TRACY'S VOICE. He's a lifeguard!
MELANIE. He's jailbait!
TRACY'S VOICE. Let me go so I can call the police. *(Caliban steps into Melanie's living room, carrying an enormous ancient book.)*
MELANIE. … All right, look, I'm hanging up now, Tracy, I'll talk to you later, okay? Bye, love you!
TRACY'S VOICE. Don't you hang up on me! Don't you dare hang up on — ! *(Melanie disconnects and she and Caliban look at each other. Caliban is tall and most definitely not misshapen. On the contrary, he's a total hunk, with long hair, broad shoulders, and veined arms. Powerful and muscular. He wears a loin-cloth-type-thing and little else. At the moment, he is dripping wet from his swim across the ocean.)*
CALIBAN. Your hair — black, like a raven's wing.
MELANIE. (Huh?) My — *what?*
CALIBAN. Your eyes — like an owl's.
MELANIE. Excuse me? *(Caliban falls to his knees before Melanie.)*
CALIBAN. Humbled, exhausted, without means, without protection, with nothing but hope, I kneel before you.
MELANIE. Hope for what?
CALIBAN. Salvation. Yours is the only magic that can crush my father's Dark Art. You are drafted in this war, raven-haired maiden with owl eyes, you must return with me to my island — you cannot shirk your duty. The Book of Destiny foretells it. *(Short pause.)*
MELANIE. Okay, you're saying things — and I'm hearing them — but I have no idea what you're talking about. Who are you?
CALIBAN. Caliban.
MELANIE. From *The Tempest?* But you're no — monster. And you're definitely not — deformed. Maybe you're Ferdinand; are

you, do you think?

CALIBAN. I *am* Caliban. I come from an island at the edge of the world. *(Short pause. Melanie takes a deep breath.)*

MELANIE. Okay, here's the short version: You're a character from a play, Caliban. (I mean, you must be.) You *think* you're alive, but you're not. You want to have fun adventures in the real world, but trust me: You'd be much happier back in your play, back on your island, which I'm sure is lovely.

CALIBAN. Once, a young woman arrived on our island's shores. Her ship had wrecked, she was the lone survivor of a cold and terrible voyage. Her name was Viola ... and like a crab, he picked the flesh from her bones and drank her blood.

MELANIE. Who did?

CALIBAN. Prospero, my father, who enslaves us, his children, with his bitter Art.

MELANIE. *(To herself.)* In *The Tempest,* Prospero's not Caliban's father ...

CALIBAN. After he was saved from drowning by a sea-witch named Sycorax, she bore him four children and taught him her magic. He mastered it, amassing it into this volume — every day becoming more and more versed in the Dark Arts, planning to return to — and destroy — Genoa.

MELANIE. *(Processing.)* Genoa? Not Milan? (Okay ...)

CALIBAN. *(Shakes his head.)* When my mother learned of his plans, she cursed Prospero. "May your feet never leave this island's yellow sands, its briny waters." So that if they ever did — immediate death. He killed her then, and has since spent every waking moment trying to unravel the curse. This very morning, he was writing in his book, perfecting the spell that would have set him free. Before he could complete it, though, I fled. I stole his book of Art, trapping him there, and I — *(A hitch in his voice.)* I've left her with him, my most precious sister Miranda.

MELANIE. Miranda's your *sister?*

CALIBAN. Miranda read in the Book of Destiny that Prospero's firstborn would arrive in the New World and ally himself with a raven-haired magician and a child-warrior. Together, they would stand against Prospero. *(Short pause.)* I am his firstborn. My sister helped me escape my chains — she unlocked their magic — and I came here. To find you.

MELANIE. What about Trincolo?

CALIBAN. Who?

MELANIE. Stephano?

CALIBAN. Lady …

MELANIE. Something's very, very wrong here; these are all characters from Shakespeare's *Tempest,* you should know them. *(Tries again:)* Ariel? *(An intake of breath, then:)*

CALIBAN. The primal annihilator, the great destroyer, yes.

MELANIE. Ariel the — the *fairy?*

CALIBAN. A hunter like no other. Savage. Ruthless. He'll cut a path of destruction as wide as the sea to find me.

MELANIE. Okay, this is New York, Caliban, I *think* we can handle a fairy. *(A knock on Melanie's apartment's front door. Uh-oh. Quoting* Macbeth:*)* "Here's a knocking indeed! If a man were porter of hell-gate, he should have plenty of practice turning the key." *(Beat.)* That's from the Scottish play. (Paraphrased, but …) *(Another knock. Melanie and Caliban turn to look at the door.)*

CALIBAN. Whenever Ariel's close to me, I can feel him tugging on my veins — like the moon pulling on the tides. I feel something, growing stronger, but faint still. *(A third knock.)*

MELANIE. You know what, I'm gonna answer that. *(Melanie goes to the door, but before she opens it, she stops. Through the door, she asks:)* Who's there? *(From the other side of the door, we hear:)*

CHET. Yeah, hi, it's me, it's Chet? *(Oh, brother.)*

MELANIE. Go — home!

CHET. Your sister called me? She said there was, like, an intruder? Maybe I can help?

MELANIE. How? You're a lifeguard, Chet. *(Beat.)* No, not even a lifeguard, a — a *li'l* lifeguard.

CHET. I promised Tracy I wouldn't go until I made sure you were all right.

MELANIE. I am, I'm fine!

CHET. I'm not going until — *(Melanie throws open the door. Chet is there, looking only a little sheepish.)*

MELANIE. Satisfied? *(Melanie opens the door wider, allowing Chet to come into her apartment. As he does so, she says:)* Chet, this is Caliban. Caliban, Chet. *(Under her breath.)* I *hate* my life.

CHET. Caliban from — from *The Tempest?*

MELANIE. No, Chet, from *The Merry Wives of Windsor.* Of course from *The Tempest. (Beat.)* I think.

CHET. *(To Caliban.)* Hi, I'm Chester Baxter. Chet Baxter.

CALIBAN. Are you a warrior?

CHET. Nah, I'm a lifeguard. But I come from a long line of war-riors. Highlanders, you know? Like in the movie with Sean Connery? And actually, I've always sorta felt like a warrior, you know? Like it's my, uhm, destiny? To fulfill?

CALIBAN. *(Realizing it.)* You *are* the child-warrior.

CHET. I mean, sure.

MELANIE. This is riveting, truly, and I wish you both could stay, I do, but a new episode of *Project Runway* starts in — *(Checks her watch.)* And I know Caliban, at least, has to be going.

CHET. *(To Caliban.)* You don't wanna hang out?

MELANIE. He can't. Apparently there's a very nasty fairy coming to hurt him.

CALIBAN. At least one, there may be others.

MELANIE. *(To Chet.)* So: Fairies, plural. And he needs to find a raven-haired magician to help him and — HEY! *(She starts snapping her fingers to remember.)* There's that magic shop on Bleecker, what's it called?

CHET. Melanie knows magic —

MELANIE. *Oh my God —*

CHET. *(To Caliban, confidentially.)* She doesn't like talking about it 'cause she has issues.

MELANIE. *Chet! (To Caliban.)* He doesn't know what he's talking about, I'm not a part of this, please go. *(Caliban sets Prospero's book on a table and opens it.)*

CALIBAN. He taught Miranda to read — but not this book.

MELANIE. Oh, for God's … *(Melanie, Chet, and Caliban gather around the book.)*

CHET. Oh, cool, look at all the — What are all those, like, symbol-things? At the top of each page?

MELANIE. I don't know, I don't even know what language this is written in — if it *is* a language. *(She turns a page, shakes her head.)* I'm sorry, Caliban, I sympathize, I do, but … I can't help you.

CALIBAN. I've risked *everything* to come here. I left Miranda alone with him. Very likely, she is already dead. This New World, your world, is in the gravest danger. If Prospero were ever to undo Sycorax's curse, he would bring the heavens down upon you. You must return to the island with me, you *and* the child-warrior.

CHET. So long as we're back for prom, I'm totally cool with whatever.

MELANIE. This has nothing to do with me!

CALIBAN. The Book of Destiny foretold that you would be reluctant, but heed me, lady: You *will* help me.

MELANIE. Are you threatening me? *(Beat.)* You're wrong. That Book of Whatever — is wrong.

CALIBAN. When the sky turns to fire and the oceans turn to blood —

MELANIE. Yadda, yadda, yadda. If Prospero's as powerful as you say he is, what could I do? My magic — *(Beat.)* You don't know my magic, it's — *(Caliban holds up the book.)*

CALIBAN. Turn his Art against him, then. Make his magic yours.

MELANIE. I can't even *read* his magic. *(Caliban holds out his arm; his hand trembles violently.)* What? What is it? Is something — ?

CALIBAN. He's not alone.

MELANIE. Who isn't? What's going — ? *(A knock on the apartment door. Uh-oh. Melanie opens her mouth to call out, but Caliban clamps his hand over it.)*

CALIBAN. *(Whispering emphatically.)* You listen to me now. If you want to live, we have to leave right now, we have to go the same way I entered your cell — through the window to the roof, do you understand? I will *not* let your pigheadedness o'errule the Book of Destiny. *(Another knock. From the hallway, we hear:)*

ARIEL'S VOICE. Brother? *(Melanie nods. Caliban releases her and as quietly as is humanly possibly — and really, they shouldn't make a sound — he, Melanie, and Chet tip-toe towards the window.)* Why do you hide from me? *(Dead silence.)* Brother? *(Chet first, then Caliban, and finally Melanie — in that order — are slipping out the window.)* I can *feel* you, Caliban. *(Melanie is almost out when she remembers:)*

MELANIE. Shit — the book! *(She starts to cross her apartment when all of a sudden — the loudest sneeze of them all.)* AH-CHOO! *(And from the other side of the door, this roaring:)*

ARIEL. CALIBAN! *(All stealth abandoned, Melanie rushes, grabs the book, and runs for the window as Ariel breaks through the door.)*

CHET. Hurry up! Hurry up!

MELANIE. *(All the while moving.)* Gogogogogo — ! *(And they're out — Melanie, Chet, and Caliban — climbing down the fire escape, just as Ariel steps into the empty apartment. Sasia follows behind him, holding up the purple flower. As she strides towards the window:)*

SASIA. Quickly! We can still — ! *(Ariel grabs her arm, stops her.)*

ARIEL. Let him run, Sasia. *(She looks at her brother.)* We've just started this game, let him go. *(Sasia is still confused.)* And when we catch him, what then? We return home, back to Father? No, let Brother run. I want to play awhile.

SASIA. The sooner we return, the sooner we'll have our freedom.

ARIEL. Do you think so? Father's made that promise before. *(Ariel releases Sasia; as she takes in Melanie's apartment:)*

SASIA. What is this cell? All these books, like Father's …

ARIEL. Is it possible he's found himself a magician? The raven-haired maiden? *(Short pause.)* Hmph. Burn it.

SASIA. What?

ARIEL. Imagine a circle as wide as our island's widest lake — with this cell at its center. *(She closes her eyes.)*

SASIA. All right, yes …

ARIEL. Now imagine everything within that circle — on fire.

SASIA. Yes …

ARIEL. This is a brave new world, Sasia. Let us fill it with terror. *(Indeed, the stage is filling with intense light as Sasia wills Melanie's apartment — and the surrounding city block — towards combustion. Before that happens, though, the lights change, and we are in a small used bookstore on Twelfth Street: Alabaster Books. Melanie, Chet, and Caliban are entering the bookstore. A little bell signals their arrival. Caliban now wears — rather absurdly — an "I heart New York" t-shirt and ill-fitting sneakers.)*

MELANIE. Thank God they're still open! *(She rings the bell on the bookstore's counter.)* Mr. Shylock? Mr. Shylock, are you back there?

CALIBAN. We cannot rest here, lady. Ariel and Sasia will hound us — they will rip us apart — to retrieve my father's book.

MELANIE. I know, I just — I'm trying to buy us some time.

CHET. Yeah, but why come here? I mean, shouldn't we be looking for a place to hide out? To, um, strategize?

MELANIE. Okay, Chet? This actually *isn't* a Playstation game. Right now, I need a bookstore. *(Gestures.)* This, Chet, is a bookstore. Amazing, right?

CHET. All right, but we passed The Strand. What's wrong with The — ?

MELANIE. Number One, you try finding something at The Strand when you're in a hurry. Number Two — *(Shylock enters from the back, wiping his hands dry.)* — Number Two, Alabaster Books is a special bookstore. *(Turns back to:)* Mr. Shylock, hi, I need a couple of plays.

SHYLOCK. How are you, my dear?

MELANIE. Good, good — uhh — a little under the gun here.

SHYLOCK. What can I get you, my darling?

MELANIE. I need a copy of *The Tempest*, if you've got it, and a copy of — uhm — actually, give me whatever Shakespeare you've got, whatever plays.

SHYLOCK. Particular imprint?

MELANIE. Hel-*lo*, the Arden.

SHYLOCK. All right, I know we don't have anything out on the floor, we're about to restock, but let me check the back. *(To Caliban.)* And for you, sir?

CALIBAN. Uhhh …

MELANIE. He's just browsing.

SHYLOCK. *(To Chet.)* And you, sir? Our Young Adult section is over by the water fountain.

CHET. Uhhh — I'm okay, thanks.

SHYLOCK. I'll just check on Mr. Shakespeare, then. *(Shylock exits. Melanie turns to Chet.)*

MELANIE. You shouldn't have come with us, Chet. You're seventeen. This is dangerous.

CALIBAN. He is the child-warrior. He is as much a part of this as you or I.

CHET. Yeah — anyway — so … how come this is a special bookstore? Is it, like, a magic bookstore? Like from *Harry Potter* or something?

MELANIE. *(Big sigh.)* It's special because Mr. Shylock — the owner — Mr. Shylock gives me books for free.

CHET. What, it's like a — sex thing?

MELANIE. *(Bigger sigh.)* When I met him, Jacob Shylock was lending money in *The Merchant of Venice*, and getting a bad rap, needless to say. But what he really wanted to do was open a bookstore, so … I set him free. That's all.

CHET. Okay, so it's not that you're into older men?

MELANIE. For Pete's sake, *no. (Chet moves away from her, browsing the stacks in the store.)*

CHET. Oh, hey, wow — look at all these old books …

CALIBAN. *(To Melanie.)* Every second we delay puts your world more at risk, lady.

MELANIE. Yeah, but Ariel's after us, right? The, uh, the primal …

CALIBAN. Annihilator, yes, the great destroyer.

MELANIE. Yeah, well, whatever he and your sister are, I'm gonna try to throw up some roadblocks. *(Under her breath.)* If I can remember how ... *(Shylock returns, bearing the Arden editions of* The Tempest, King Lear, *and* Coriolanus.*)*

SHYLOCK. I don't have much, I'm afraid: *The Tempest* — we got that, at least — and *King Lear* ...

CHET. Hey, that's my favorite — I played Gloucester in eighth grade.

SHYLOCK. ... and *Coriolanus.*

MELANIE. *(Taking the books.)* Oh, Mr. Shylock, thank you, you're a *dream. Coriolanus* — it's perfect!

SHYLOCK. So I'm a dream tonight? All right, I can live with that. Can the dream do anything else for you or can he close up now?

MELANIE. Actually — *(She passes Prospero's book to Shylock.)* could you maybe, uhm, appraise this book for us? For me? *(Shylock holds the book up, feels its weight in his hands.)*

SHYLOCK. My glasses are in the back ...

MELANIE. Take your time. *(Once Shylock has exited.)* Okay, let's see here. *(Melanie starts flipping through the Arden* Tempest, *stops when she finds a picture.)* Okay, all right. *(She tears the page with the picture out.)*

CHET. Whoa.

MELANIE. I know. We don't normally do that to books but in this case — *(Turns to Caliban, holds up the picture.)* Is this your brother? Is this Ariel?

CALIBAN. One of his guises, yes. Where did you — ? *(But Melanie is already onto the next. She takes the copy of* Coriolanus, *kneels down on the floor. As she does:)*

MELANIE. Caius Marcius Coriolanus, the greatest of Shakespeare's warriors, who single-handedly defeated the entire Volscian army. *(Beat.)* Dumb as a stick and a total mama's boy. If anyone can run interference for us, *he* can. *(Melanie spreads the play flat, holding it open with her palms. She closes her eyes and starts concentrating, but almost immediately —)*

CHET. Wait, are you doing it? Like, right now? Are you — ?

MELANIE. My heart's racing and my palms are sweating and my stomach's in a knot. The last time I did this — *(She closes her eyes again, resumes concentrating.)* It's like ... opening ... a ... door ... Like ... *(But Melanie slams* Coriolanus *shut.)* It's no use! I can't — I can't do this! *(To Caliban.)* The Book of Destiny is wrong. I'm *not* the raven-haired maiden, I'm just some over-educated, under-employed drama — *(Caliban lays a hand on Melanie's shoulder.)*

CALIBAN. The Book of Destiny was written at the dawn of time, it is *never* wrong. Steady yourself. Be the eye of the storm. All your life has been leading to this moment. *(Melanie looks at Caliban.)*

MELANIE. Do you know what the consequences — ?

CALIBAN. There is none alive who knows the consequences of magic ill-used more than me. *(Beat.)* And nothing you could set free, lady, would be worse than what pursues us. *(Melanie shakes her head, but closes her eyes and returns to the book. Again, she lays her palms on its pages and starts whispering.)*

MELANIE. Like … opening … a … door. Picturing it in my head … and … watching … it … swing … open? *(A moment passes, and another. Melanie opens her eyes. Silence in the bookshop. Then:)*

CHET. Did it work? Did it happen? *(More silence. Then — although the shop's door doesn't open — we hear the sound of that little bell ringing.)*

MELANIE. *(Terrified.)* Oh my God. Oh … my … God.

CHET. What?

MELANIE. Don't say anything — for the next three minutes, okay? *(She turns to Caliban, as she pulls her hair back severely to look mean and school-marmish.)* You wanted a warrior? *(A shadow, as someone emerges from behind the stacks. Whoever he is, he's powerful and enormous, almost seven feet tall. He wears a breastplate and helmet. His jaw is square, his face scarred. He is the greatest Roman gladiator in the canon. Melanie calls him by his full name.)* Caius Marcius!

MARCIUS. Here!

MELANIE. Who's a naughty boy, then?

MARCIUS. Ma'am?

MELANIE. Show me your hands, Caius Marcius. *(Indeed, Marcius has been keeping his hands folded behind his back. He brings them out slowly. They are, no surprise, dripping blood.)*

MARCIUS. I didn't mean to.

MELANIE. *(Sighing.)* Who was it this time?

MARCIUS. The … the …

MELANIE. DON'T LIE TO ME!

MARCIUS. Ma'am, the Roman tribunes, ma'am, they called me names!

MELANIE. And you attacked them. That was very *bad*, Caius Marcius, very, very *childish*.

MARCIUS. Please don't tell my mother!

MELANIE. Oh, Caius, I'm afraid I have to —

MARCIUS. *(Dropping to his knees.)* OHPLEASENO.

MELANIE. Unless, perhaps …

MARCIUS. YES — GODS — YES — ANYTHING. *(Melanie holds up the picture of Ariel.)*

MELANIE. This man has insulted your mother's honor — *(Caius reacts.)* Yes, that's right — and is at this very moment roaming the city streets. Can you stop him, do you think? Using *extreme* prejudice? *(Marcius takes the picture of Ariel, slowly smiles, and bows his head.)*

MARCIUS. Ma'am … he is a tiger I am proud to hunt.

MELANIE. Don't let his looks fool you. He's very strong, very dangerous.

CALIBAN. Both Ariel *and* my sister Sasia.

MARCIUS. However many stand with him, I'll make a quarry of them, as high as I can pick my lance.

MELANIE. I'm counting on it. *(He starts out again.)* Caius Marcius, one last thing!

MARCIUS. Ma'am?

MELANIE. He called you … *a boy of tears. (With that, Marcius' face darkens, he crumples the picture of Ariel in his hand, and strides out the door.)*

CALIBAN. I fear you've sent him to his grave, lady. *(Melanie is stone-faced.)*

MELANIE. Let's not go there, okay? *(She tosses him* The Tempest.*)* Here, see if any of the other pictures in there mean anything to you. *(The enormity of what she's just done hits her.)* Oh, God …

CHET. Are you okay?

MELANIE. I promised myself I'd never do that again. *(Turns to Chet.)* No, Chet, I am most definitely *not* okay.

CHET. Yeah, but that guy, he was like — that guy was like — *(Caliban, who has been flipping through* The Tempest, *stops at another picture: the Fuseli painting.)*

CALIBAN. These people — *(He points them out.)* — my father. And my sister … *(Melanie goes to him.)*

MELANIE. Is that them? Is that what they look like?

CALIBAN. Yes, but — *(He points to another figure in the painting.)* — what is this monster? This twisted, humped horror … *(Melanie looks. Silence for a bit.)*

MELANIE. Caliban, that's — that's you. *(Confused, Caliban looks at Melanie.)*

CALIBAN. How can this be?

MELANIE. *(Realizing it.)* Oh, God. You're … *not* from a play, are you? You're … real.

CHET. Wait, what?

MELANIE. *(To Caliban.)* Somehow … you're real. Not just Prospero … all of you. Shakespeare must've based *all* of you on real people … *(Shylock returns, rubbing his chin, sets Prospero's book on the counter.)*

SHYLOCK. Melanie, dear, this book is a conundrum. I couldn't even begin to guess how much it's worth, but it's not nothing.

MELANIE. Do you know what it's written in? What language?

SHYLOCK. No, but I got a friend at Columbia, she studies ancient languages, ancient texts, magic, you name it. Give her a call, maybe she can help. Here — *(He hands Melanie a piece of paper with this gal's name and phone number on it.)* her name's Linda Summers. A real crackerjack. Call her tonight, she's a graduate student, she never sleeps.

MELANIE. Thank you, Mr. Shylock, I'll do that.

SHYLOCK. Oh, there's also this flower. *(He takes the pressed flower from the pages of the book.)* Had you seen this?

MELANIE. No. *(She looks to Caliban, who shakes his head.)* No, we hadn't.

SHYLOCK. If you want, I got a lady friend coming over later tonight —

CHET. Score.

SHYLOCK. *(To Chet.)* Yeah, I wish. She's just a friend, an acquaintance. But she knows about flowers — more than I do, even. *(Holding the flower:)* Can I keep this? Just for tonight?

MELANIE. Oh, Mr. Shylock, you're an angel — thank you. *(She takes the book from the counter, turns to go.)* Thanks. I'll call you tomorrow about the flower.

SHYLOCK. That's fine. *(As Chet, Caliban, and Melanie head out.)* Oh, Melanie, one more thing.

MELANIE. Sure.

SHYLOCK. That book, its cover? I don't think it's leather.

MELANIE. Oh? *(Almost instinctively, Melanie turns to Caliban.)*

CALIBAN. *(To Melanie.)* The skin of the girl who shipwrecked …

MELANIE. Mr. Shylock, we — we gotta go. Thanks, thank you, I'll call you tomorrow.

SHYLOCK. All right, yes, have fun tonight. And keep cool. People are dying over this heat. *(The three adventurers leave. Shylock locks his shop's front door, hears fire engines as they pass, their red lights flashing. Shaking his head sadly, Shylock moves back into his shop, adjusts the lights for his big date, turns on the radio. A lilting melody starts to play.)*

Shylock goes into the back room of his shop, comes out with plates and silverware for dinner. He arranges the dinner stuff on his counter, picks up the flower, smells it — frowns — and hears: A knock on his shop's door. We see the shadow of someone waiting outside.) Wilhelmina? Is that you? *(Another knock.)* All right, hold your horses, I'm coming, I'm coming ... *(He approaches the door, but before he gets to it, Ariel and Sasia burst through it, striding into the shop.)* I'm sorry, we're clo —

ARIEL. Where is the book?

SHYLOCK. Wh-which book is that?

ARIEL. *(Turning to:)* Sasia?

SASIA. They *were* here, brother.

ARIEL. *(Returning to Shylock.)* Where did they go?

SHYLOCK. Wh-who?

ARIEL. Every time you make me repeat myself, old man, I will carve a pound of flesh from your body until there is nothing left but bone and sinew and nerve. *Where did they go?* My brother Caliban and the raven-haired maiden?

SHYLOCK. I — I don't know what you're talking about.

SASIA. Then let us explain it to him, brother — *(She smiles wickedly.)* very — *very* — slowly. *(Ariel and Sasia crowd around Shylock, but before we see what they do to him, the shop darkens to only a pinpoint of light ... which widens to reveal Prospero's island again. Miranda runs on, being pursued by Prospero. She stumbles and falls; he looms over her like a threatening giant.)*

PROSPERO. I'll ask you once more, Daughter: Did you help your brother escape? *(Silence.)* Caliban's chains were held together with an incantation, locked by runes. Only a spell, read aloud, could have freed your brother.

MIRANDA. Stop this, Father — please — I beg you. Before your soul becomes so twisted — your heart so hardened — that there is no way —

PROSPERO. WE ARE DISCUSSING CALIBAN!

MIRANDA. *(Yelling back.)* WHY DOES HE TERRIFY YOU? *(Beat.)* Of all your children? What power does he have over you?

PROSPERO. *(Chuckling to himself.)* You ask me of power, Daughter? *(Beat.)* When my power, my Art, is all that keeps your brother human? *(Miranda's confused.)* Have you never wondered why I call Caliban misshapen? A monster? *(Beat.)* It is because I call him what he is *beneath* his skin. More than any of you, Caliban is his mother's son. A half-breed, a mutt, a mongrel. Who looks human because *I* will it so. *(Beat as Prospero decides something.)* But no longer …

MIRANDA. Father …

PROSPERO. You try to protect your brother from me, but you cannot protect someone from what is within. *(Prospero holds his right hand out before him. He starts to flex it slowly, opening and closing it.)* From this moment on, Caliban is released. Let a sea-change occur, let him return to what he once was — half-man, half-beast — a *true* thing of darkness — and let us see who has power over whom. *(A crash of lightning accompanies the completion of the spell Prospero is casting. The thunder from the lightning segues into the disco favorite "It's Raining Men" and … we're on a stage in an after-hours nightclub. Three fabulous, appropriately outfitted drag queens — Tisiphone, Megaera, and Alecto — enter with plastic, see-through umbrellas. They are rehearsing their act; lip-synching and dancing to the song. A few moments into their act, Melanie bursts in. She tries to get Tisiphone's attention.)*

MELANIE. Tisiphone! Tisiphone! Over here! *(Finally, Melanie sneezes — and Tisiphone stops dancing, signals for Megaera and Alecto to stop. Tisiphone snaps her fingers and the music cuts off.)*

TISIPHONE. *(Without turning to look at her.)* This is a closed rehearsal. Club Dionysus won't open for —

MELANIE. Tisiphone, it's me, it's Melanie!

TISIPHONE. Melanie? *(Remembering, turning to her.)* Melanie! In that case, let me slip into something a little more *me*. *(Tisiphone and the other two drag queens rip off their costumes in a flourish, revealing warrior garb from Ancient Greece and hair full of writhing snakes.)*

MELANIE. Exactly! I need your help, Tisiphone! The kind of help only a Fury can provide!

TISIPHONE. Tell me, I'll all ears. *(Caliban bursts into the room. Tisiphone eyes him up and down. She's impressed.)* Well, not *all* ears.

MELANIE. We need sanctuary — protection — while I … figure some things out. *(Chet bursts in, still carrying his orange life-preserver. Tisiphone looks Chet up and down.)*

TISIPHONE. *(To Melanie.)* And who's this? Your intern?

CHET. Hey, is there a bathroom here? You know, a men's room?

TISIPHONE. *(To Chet.)* All we have here are men's rooms. Allow me —

MELANIE. *(Stepping between them.)* He's seventeen, Tisiphone.

TISIPHONE. Hey. If he's old enough to pee —

MELANIE. *(To Chet, pointing offstage.)* Down the hall, around the partition, all the way in the back. *(Beat.)* Hurry.

CHET. Cool, thanks.

MELANIE. Wait. Leave the book with me.

CHET. Sure — *(Holds up the orange life-saving device.)* It's in here. *(Gives it to her.)* High-density plastic *and* it's waterproof. *(Chet goes.)*

TISIPHONE. *(To Melanie, regarding Chet, smiling.)* He's an orphan. He tried to pick your pocket. Rather than turn him over to child services, you decided to adopt. *(Turns to Caliban.)* He comes with his own personal trainer.

MELANIE. We're on the run, Tisiphone. We need a place to hide, to — regroup. And you owe me. You've owed me ever since I set you and your ... back-up Furies free from The *Oresteia*. *(Tisiphone turns to Megaera and Alecto.)*

TISIPHONE. Ladies — five minutes. Attend to ...

MELANIE. Caliban. *(Tisiphone does a double-take, but turns back to the hunk.)*

TISIPHONE. You look tired and hungry. Let's see what my sisters can do to freshen you up a bit. *(To her singers.)* Complete make-over.

CALIBAN. For your hospitality, many thanks, lady. *(Tisiphone looks at Melanie, who shrugs. Alecto and Megaera approach Caliban.)*

ALECTO. Handsome man ...

MEGAERA. More than man and less ...

ALECTO. The difference between ...

MEGAERA. ... the difference between ...

ALECTO. ... between man and man. *(As they start to lead him offstage.)*

MEGAERA. We'll soothe you ...

ALECTO. And bathe you ...

MEGAERA. And dress you ...

ALECTO. And feed you ...

MEGAERA. And soothe you ...

ALECTO. *(Annoyed, to Megaera.)* You said "soothe" already. *(They are gone. Tisiphone raises an eyebrow to Melanie, who shrugs again.)*

MELANIE. That's me, Melanie Porter, putting the "drama" in "dramaturg" one script at a time ...

TISIPHONE. Caliban?

MELANIE. Yeah, but not from Shakespeare's play.

TISIPHONE. *(Bitchy.)* From where, then — Chelsea?

MELANIE. No, listen, I've been thinking about this. Prospero, Ariel, Caliban — the people Shakespeare based *The Tempest* on — they're real, Tisiphone, they're *alive*. They've been alive all this time.

TISIPHONE. Which would make them — what, almost five hundred years old?

MELANIE. So? *You're* immortal.

TISIPHONE. Yeah, but that's *me.*

MELANIE. Can you be serious, please? *(Tisiphone zips her lips.)* Caliban says his father, brother, and sister are trying to kill him. He says my magic is the only thing that can help him. He says he wants me to go back with him — back to their island. To, uhm, face Prospero.

TISIPHONE. *(Unzipping.)* Which you're not going to do.

MELANIE. *(Emphatically.)* No, absolutely not, no way. *(Mini-pause.)* I don't know, maybe. *(Short pause.)* This sounds crazy, I know, but I've dreamt about him, Tisiphone. Many, many times. *(Caliban returns, followed by Alecto and Megaera.)*

TISIPHONE. So what, I've dreamt about Russell Crowe many, many times, but that doesn't mean I owe him anything. *(A hand on Melanie's shoulder.)* I know you, Melanie, I know what you are capable of — and what you are not. You're not going to any island. Which, for all we know, doesn't exist.

CALIBAN. It does, believe me. *(All eyes turn to Caliban.)* It was an earthly paradise, a place like no other, full of sounds and sights and sweet airs that gave delight. Now it is frozen, out of time, and only Prospero's defeat will restore it.

MELANIE. *(To Tisiphone.)* You hear that? Frozen — out of time.

TISIPHONE. *(To Caliban.)* You listen to me, Jungle Boy, she's not going *anywhere* with you. She will *never* deliver the kind of magic you need to fight Prospero. Not because she can't, you understand, but because she won't let herself. Because she doesn't have the *stuff* for it. *(Beat.)* And even if she did, you think I'd let her risk her life for you?

CALIBAN. *(To Melanie.)* We stand together against him, lady. Your magic against his.

TISIPHONE. Shut up. You don't know *anything* about her magic.

CALIBAN. I know that balladeers will write songs about her feats one day. I know that stars will be named after her. The greatest magician of them all —

TISIPHONE. Oh, *please.* You think I'm gonna let her run off and get herself killed on some fucking island? Because what happens to *me,* then? I get sucked back into The *Oresteia,* that's what, and I don't *think* so. Sugar hasn't worked her fingers to the bone to build a life here just so *you* can put it at risk. *(Beat.)* We're depending on

28

her, everyone she's set free, accidentally or otherwise, to keep us alive, to keep us in the here and now.

CALIBAN. Nothing will happen to her. I protect her. The child-warrior protects her. The Book of Destiny —

TISIPHONE. You have no idea what you're asking her to do. That, or you don't care. Why should she put her life in danger to help you? Why should she — ?

MELANIE. *(Interrupting.)* Stop it, Tisiphone — *(Includes Caliban.)* Both of you, please! *(They do stop. Then:)*

TISIPHONE. You better tell him, Melanie. *(Emphatically.)* And not that cock-and-bull story about Romeo and Tybalt. *(At that, Melanie slowly turns to Caliban, lays it down for him.)*

MELANIE. *(To Caliban.)* Caliban, I — I can't go with you. Whatever you think I'm capable of … I'm not. Whatever you think my magic can do … *(She shakes her head.)* I freed Coriolanus because he's one-dimensional and I could — *direct* him, but anyone more willful, more unpredictable, and …

CALIBAN. What, lady? What terrifies you so?

MELANIE. I tried to save a little girl once. Her name was Iphigeneia. She was going to be sacrificed to win a war, so I … set her free from her play and … someone terrible got out, too. The man who was trying to kill her, Agamemnon, her father … And when I tried to keep her from him, he started … terrorizing the city. Going after children — little girls. Hurting them. He was going to kill them in Iphigeneia's place — he would have, too, if …

TISIPHONE. If you hadn't set *us* free to intervene: The Furies. The Greek spirits of vengeance and justice. *(Beat.)* Oooo, you *hated* me when I handed her over to him. I'll never forget that look in your face. *(Beat.)* You were fourteen. You were trying to save a girl from her destiny, but — you — couldn't.

MELANIE. No … *(Shaking her head at the memory.)* And I'll never forget the wind that blew through the city the night Agamemnon took Iphigeneia away, back to Aulis, back to her death, and I gave up my magic.

CALIBAN. Your fear is what will make you great.

MELANIE. No. I should have told you from the start. I shouldn't have given you hope. I — I'm sorry. *(The moment holds for a few beats. Until Chet returns, seriously dazed and confused — in a trance.)*

CHET. It's okay … we don't have to worry … anymore …

MELANIE. Chet?

CHET. No, I mean it … I talked to her, it's totally arranged …
(Caliban holds up his arm — it's shaking.) All we have to do is give
them back the book … which doesn't even really belong to us …
MELANIE. Talked to whom, Chet?
CHET. This woman … this beautiful woman …
CALIBAN. Sasia is part siren. She can muddy men's minds.
MELANIE. Who? *(From the club's shadows, Sasia steps into the
light. She is carrying an enormous Bloomingdale's bag.)*
SASIA. What a tricksy chase you've led us on, Brother. *(Melanie,
meantime, goes to Chet.)*
MELANIE. Chet, are you — ? Look at me, Chet, focus on my —
SASIA. I told Ariel: Flower or no flower, once I've picked up a
person's scent, there's none can hide from me.
CHET. *(Drowsily.)* M-Melanie …
SASIA. Father's book of Art, Caliban — now.
MELANIE. Wake up, Chet. Wake — up —
CHET. I'm awake, I'm awake …
SASIA. Who are these creatures you've surrounded yourself with?
Whose lives you play with?
MELANIE. *(To Sasia.)* I sent someone after you — Caius Marcius
— a warrior —
SASIA. Did you? Then let me return — *(She reaches into the
Bloomingdale's bag, pulls out Caius Marcius' bloody severed head.)* He
might've defeated the Volscian army, but he wouldn't have lasted a
week in father's salt mines. *(She tosses the head to Melanie and Chet,
who catches it.)*
CHET. Mel …
MELANIE. Start backing away, Chet — very, *very* slowly …
CALIBAN. You're not alone, Sasia, where is Ariel? *(From thin air,
a disembodied voice:)*
ARIEL'S VOICE. Behind you, Brother. *(The sound of someone
being struck, and Caliban reels, as though he has been punched across
the jaw — which he has, by the invisible Ariel.)*
MELANIE. Caliban, what's — ? *(Another smack. Caliban staggers.
His mouth is bleeding.)* Stop it! What are you doing to him?
SASIA. You — raven-haired maiden or whoever you are — that's
enough from you.
MELANIE. Chet, get out of here! *Take your preserver* and get out
of here — *right* — now. *(Chet takes a beat, looks at Melanie, grabs
his orange life-preserver, then bolts from the club. Caliban is hit a third*

time. He starts swinging madly.)

CALIBAN. Show yourself, coward! Show yourself!

SASIA. *(Advancing on Melanie.)* I burned your cell —

MELANIE. My what?

SASIA. — now, I'll burn you, as well. *(Ariel materializes behind Caliban. He grabs him in a stranglehold.)*

ARIEL. The book, Caliban, or we'll kill them all, beginning with — *(White light is building up around Melanie.)*

MELANIE. Why is it so — *hot?*

CALIBAN. Release her, Sasia —

ARIEL. The book, Brother —

MELANIE. Tisiphone, a little help here …

TISIPHONE. You know the rules, love, the Furies can only intervene in matters of blood, in feuds between relations.

MELANIE. They are — (oh, God) — they *are* related!

TISIPHONE. *(Intrigued.)* Are they? In that case — *(Turns to:)* Alecto. Megaera. *(Alecto and Megaera move in behind Tisiphone. A club remix of a song like Donna Summer's "Bad Girls" starts to play.*)*

ALECTO. Older than the Earth …

MEGAERA. Older than the gods …

ALECTO. Before time …

MEGAERA. When there was nothing …

TISIPHONE. *We* were there.

ALECTO. Alecto.

TISIPHONE. "Unceasing in Pursuit." *(Alecto unsheathes a sword hidden in her umbrella's handle.)*

MEGAERA. Megaera.

ALECTO. "The Envious Rager." *(Megaera unsheathes a sword hidden in her umbrella's handle.)*

TISIPHONE. Tisiphone.

MEGAERA and ALECTO. "The Blood Avenger." *(Tisiphone unsheathes a sword hidden in her umbrella's handle.)*

TISIPHONE. The immortal daughters of Mother Earth, sprung from the blood of Kronus, existing out of time …

MEGAERA. Across time …

ALECTO. Those Who Walk in Darkness …

MEGAERA. The Dirae …

ALECTO. The Eumenides …

TISIPHONE. The Kindly Ones …

---

* See Special Note on Songs and Recordings on copyright page.

ALL. The *Furies.*

TISIPHONE. Let them go or we'll rip you apart. *(A showdown. The white light around Melanie begins to fade. Sasia is beginning to doubt.)*

SASIA. Brother…? *(Ariel and Tisiphone's eyes are locked. Neither will back down.)*

ARIEL. Burn her.

MELANIE. What?

ARIEL. I'll wager our father's magic, his protection, against these *women.* Burn the bookish one from her innards out, starting with her heart. *(The white light starts building up around Melanie again.)*

MELANIE. Tisiphone … *(Ariel releases Caliban, pushing him to the ground. Caliban starts back up, but Ariel strikes him across the face, keeping him down. Ariel turns to face Tisiphone.)*

ARIEL. You call yourselves Furies? *(Chet runs back on, carrying Prospero's book in one arm, a lit flare in the other, which he brandishes like a torch.)*

CHET. EVERYONE STOP OR I'LL BURN PROSPERO'S BOOK! *(Silence. Chet continues:)* This is a standard, Coast Guard-issued signal flare. It burns hot, over a thousand degrees. On a clear night, you can see it almost a mile away. I don't care if the book's magic or not, it's still paper, it'll still burn. *(Beat.)* Stop what you're doing.

SASIA. Ariel? *(Chet brings the book and the flare closer together.)*

CHET. I mean it, I'll do it.

ARIEL. Hold, sister. *(The white light around Melanie goes out. She falls to her knees, panting, drenched in sweat.)*

CHET. Your father sent you after Caliban, but really it's the book he cares about, am I right? *(Continues quickly.)* It's okay, you don't have to answer, I know I am. *(Beat.)* So — yeah — anyway — you'd better go now before my arms get tired and I have to set these two things down on top of one another. *(Ariel takes a step towards Chet.)* Back — off — now. *(Ariel stops.)*

SASIA. Like us, the book is enchanted — protected. You cannot harm it.

CHET. Yeah? *(Chet drops to his knees, slams the book open, rips a page out of it — reaction from everyone in the room — Chet touches the page to the flare. It burns, flames licking up the side of it.)* Who knows what that spell was for. *(The page is blackened ash, drifting up around them.)*

ARIEL. Little man, you have no idea what you've done, what your torments will be —

CHET. Yeahyeahyeah. Don't make me do another page. Go.

CALIBAN. And tell Father to prepare. The wheel of fortune turns, the prophecy will be fulfilled, his day of reckoning approaches.

ARIEL. You'll see him soon yourself. On your knees, begging for mercy. *(He looks around the room.)* You'll all die.

TISIPHONE. Not me, baby, I live forever.

ARIEL. *All* of you … *(Ariel and Sasia start backing away, retreating into the club's shadows. Caliban holds out his arm. It is shaking, but steadying, steadying, steadying, until it is still.)*

TISIPHONE. And the bad guys have left the building. *(Looking around.)* Who wants a cocktail? *(The two back-up furies raise their hands; Chet, meantime, is still holding the burning flare.)*

CHET. Great, so can anyone…?

ALECTO. Over here, Tiny. *(Alecto takes the flare, exits with it — as do Tisiphone and Megaera.)*

MELANIE. Chet … *(Melanie pulls herself up.)*

CHET. Are you okay? *(She takes a step towards Chet.)*

MELANIE. The book, Chet …

CHET. Oh, that? That wasn't Prospero's book. This is Prospero's book. *(He opens his orange life-saving device, pulls out Prospero's book.)* What I burned, it's an Olde English Dictionary. (You know, the O.E.D.?) When we were at Mr. Shylock's bookstore, I saw it, and thought we might — That maybe it would — I thought: Maybe I should take it in case —

MELANIE. Chet … *(She is right in front of Chet.)*

CHET. What, was that bad?

MELANIE. Don't say anything, okay? For the next thirty seconds, don't talk.

CHET. How come? *(Melanie kisses Chet on the mouth. Eventually, both of them embarrassed, they break apart, and:)*

MELANIE. I'm — uh — gonna call Mr. Shylock's graduate student friend.

CHET. Yeah, cool, and I should probably call my — *(Sheepishly.)* mom. *(Melanie exits and Chet takes out a cell phone, dials. Caliban, meanwhile, sits off to the side, hugging himself.)*

CHET. Hi, Mom, yeah, it's me … At a club, in the backroom of some dance club … I know it's late, Ma, but I didn't want you to worry … Yes, I'm keeping cool. Yes, even in this heat … Oh, it was fine. Pretty much like every other date … Maybe, hopefully, I'd like to … Yeah, I will, I promise. *(Beat.)* Yeah, I love you, too. *(Chet hangs up.)*

CALIBAN. You are fortunate, to have a family that cares for you.

CHET. It's … just my mom and me now. My dad — he was a life-guard, too — he died. *(Nods his head.)* Yeah, a kid was trapped down in an underwater cave beneath a boulder-type-thing, and my dad was trying to pull him free and … he drowned. *(Beat.)* He saved him, though, the kid.

CALIBAN. He died a hero, then.

CHET. Uhm, we never thought about him like that, and *he* definitely didn't, but yeah … I guess he was. *(Beat.)* That's partly how come my mom worries so much.

CALIBAN. I never had that.

CHET. Not even — wait — not even from your own mother?

CALIBAN. From Miranda. We'd hold each other, cowering, while Father raged like a storm. She would say to me: "One day, brother, he will be gone from our lives, and we will sit by the calm ocean, under a sky that never clouds, and we will read, and play chess, and swim, and be — free."

CHET. It'll happen. You'll see. *(Melanie returns, shutting a cell phone as she comes in.)*

MELANIE. Okay, I just talked to Mr. Shylock's friend at Columbia. Linda Summers, the ancient languages expert or whatever? She's grading papers, working late, but she can see me tonight if I go right now.

CHET. Great. *(Beat.)* And — uhm — remind me why that's a good thing.

MELANIE. Maybe she'll know how to destroy the book? Or maybe she knows where we can find a real magician? *(Turns to:)* Caliban, I'm in this now, okay? You're not alone. I don't know what I can do, but whatever I can, I will. I'll see this through, as much as possible. *(She pulls an old-fashioned and terrifying pistol from her bag, checks to see if it's loaded.)*

CHET. Uhm. What is that?

MELANIE. The only pistol I could get my hands on.

CHET. From where?

MELANIE. *Annie Get Your Gun.* One of the Furies is auditioning for it. *(Holds up the gun to show Caliban.)* What do you think, Caliban, I know it's not magic, but — *(Melanie stops, notices Caliban is starting to convulse.)* What? What's wrong?

CALIBAN. Something … happening to me …

MELANIE. What, Caliban? My God, you're shaking.

CALIBAN. I d-don't — *(Caliban holds up his hand, clenched into a fist. He starts flexing it open. His hand is webbed now, amphibian.)*

MELANIE. Oh, my God. *(Caliban takes off his shirt. He twists around to see — and so the audience can see — his back. There are shark-like fins running down his spine.)*

CHET. Oh, wow.

MELANIE. Okay — nobody panic.

CALIBAN. My father's magic …

CHET. I think you look — you know — totally cool. *(Tisiphone enters, a grim expression on her face.)*

CALIBAN. My mother … part sea-devil …

MELANIE. Oh, God, on top of everything else!

TISIPHONE. It gets worse. I just consulted the Oracle.

CHET. The what?

TISIPHONE. Of Delphi. To see if I could learn anything, to see how this all turns out, and …

MELANIE. What?

TISIPHONE. The Oracle couldn't see how it ends precisely. But it did show me …

MELANIE. What, Tisiphone?

TISIPHONE. The city — this city — in flames. Blood in the streets. People dying.

MELANIE. Oh, God. Because of — because of Sasia and Ariel?

TISIPHONE. And Prospero. *(Beat.)* The Oracle told me: He comes to New York.

MELANIE. What? That's impossible, Sycorax's curse — *(Confused, turning to Caliban.)* What does that mean? Caliban, what does that — ?

TISIPHONE. It means you *will* face him, Melanie. All three of you will. *(A flourish.)* Four, if you count me.

MELANIE. If…? *(She nods.)* Thanks, thank you.

TISIPHONE. Don't thank me yet. I have a terrible presentiment not all of us are gonna make it through the night. *(Caliban's breathing is heavy. He, Melanie, and Chet look at each other. They don't know what to say. The lights start fading to black.)*

End of Act One

ACT TWO

A spot of light on a hand, clutching an impressive, rocky, ancient-looking spear. The spot widens to reveal: Tisiphone, holding the spear, with Melanie, Chet, and Caliban — looking a little more lizard-ish — standing nearby, still in Club Dionysus.

TISIPHONE. *(With awe.)* The spear of destiny. One of the most powerful weapons in the known universe.

CHET. Actually, isn't that technically a spear*head*? Shouldn't it be called the spearhead of destiny? I mean, a spear's a long, skinny weapon, and that's just — *(Tisiphone and Melanie look at Chet.)* anyway ...

TISIPHONE. It is one of four spears carved from the meteorite that started the first Ice Age. Three of the spears were cast into the sea, where (for all I know) they still are, being pulled back and forth by the tides, carving grooves in the ocean's floor. But this last one ... Cain used it to murder his brother Abel. A Roman Centurion used it to pierce the side of a condemned man named Jesus. Constantine the Great carried it into battle, as did Charlemagne. Napoleon had it, then lost it.

CHET. Where?

MELANIE. Waterloo.

TISIPHONE. Apparently, it's *not* just an ABBA song.

CALIBAN. I have heard stories of a magic spear. Once, in the highlands, a dread general — and his fiend-like wife — used it to a murder a king. Its influence destroyed them both.

CHET. And — so — is that a copy?

TISIPHONE. No, cupcake. Here, touch it, feel its power. *(Tisiphone gives Chet the spear.)* Can you?

CHET. *(Dubious.)* Uhm, I guess?

CALIBAN. Will it ... kill my father?

TISIPHONE. It tears through magic — tears through anything. *(Beat.)* Of course, it means getting close enough to use it.

36

CALIBAN. We will. *(Reaching for the spear.)* Give it to me, child-warrior, and I will deliver the killing blow. *(As Chet steps out of Caliban's reach:)*

CHET. Actually, don't you think maybe I should? I mean, he'll be expecting it from you, won't he? You can, I don't know … *distract* him.

MELANIE. Which should be easy, considering the fact that you're turning into the *Creature from the Black Lagoon. (Beat.)* No offense.

TISIPHONE. *(To Melanie.)* Perhaps Caliban should lie down, don't you think — rest up? I have a cot in the next room. *(Beat, she winks at Caliban.)* Big enough for two.

MELANIE. *(Shaking her head.)* No, we — we should keep moving, we have to be ready, we have to plan. The spear's good thinking, Tisiphone. And I'm going uptown to see what I can learn about Prospero's book —

CHET. I still don't get why. The Book of Destiny said *your* magic would defeat Prospero. It didn't say anything about using Prospero's magic against him. *(Silence for a beat, then:)*

MELANIE. *(Bitchy, bitchy.)* I'm sorry, Tisiphone, did you hear anything?

TISIPHONE. Nope.

MELANIE. Yeah, me, neither.

CHET. Jeez, sorry for trying to contribute.

MELANIE. Unfortunately, Chet, unless you know how to change Caliban back —

CALIBAN. *(Ominous, ominous.)* I *like* what I'm becoming … *(Tisiphone, Melanie, and Chet exchange a nervous look.)*

TISIPHONE. Nevertheless, I think I know where I can get something that will help slow down — maybe even reverse — your changing. *(Checking in with Melanie.)* If we have time.

MELANIE. We'll make it. *(To Caliban.)* We'll need you at a hundred percent for whatever happens when Prospero gets here.

CHET. Which makes me, like — what, totally superfluous? *(To Melanie.)* I'm supposed to be protecting you.

MELANIE. Actually … How well do you know New York, Chet?

CHET. Uhm …

MELANIE. Let me rephrase that: well enough to hide a man-sized iguana from his father? *(Chet assesses the situation.)*

CHET. Not a problem.

MELANIE. Great — you're up, then. And Tisiphone's given us all these fashionable cell phones, right? — *(They check; they have them.)*

so we'll keep in touch that way. *(Turns to Chet.)* As soon as you know where you're going, call or text and we'll rendezvous in … an hour?

CHET. Check.

TISIPHONE. *(Fixing her eyes on Caliban.)* Are you *sure* you're all right, Caliban

CALIBAN. Never … stronger …

CHET. *(Aside.)* Uhm. Melanie?

MELANIE. Yes, Chet?

CHET. Before I go, can I — uhm — give you something?

MELANIE. Uh …

CHET. Here — *(Taking it off.)* It's my dad's whistle.

MELANIE. Oh, Chet — *(He gives it to her.)* Uh …

CHET. If you're in trouble, you can blow on it, and no matter where I am, I'll hear it, and I'll come running, okay?

MELANIE. Oh, Chet, you really don't have to —

CHET. I want to. *(Hello! Melanie looks at Chet — has a moment — and then puts the whistle around her neck.)*

MELANIE. … Thank you, Chet.

CHET. You're welcome. *(Beat.)* Yeah, okay, so — uhm — do I get another kiss?

MELANIE. Excuse me?

CHET. You know, like before?

MELANIE. What? *(Remembering.)* Oh, Chet, that was — that was a token, a gesture. *(Beat.)* What did you think, that we were dating? *Going steady?*

CHET. Uhm, well, I guess —

MELANIE. It was nothing, you dope. Honestly, another kiss. Get out of here, you're such a dope.

CHET. I wasn't thinking, I guess. I'm sorry.

MELANIE. Get going, you dope. And stay — *(Her mask slips a bit.)* Stay safe, all right? Hug the darkness, stick to the alleys and piers.

CHET. Oh, don't worry about me. I'm the child-warrior, remember? *(Chet and Caliban go, Melanie looking after them. Slowly, she puts her face in her hands, shakes her head. She won't cry. She won't let herself cry.)*

TISIPHONE. It's okay, the bravado. Pretend you don't care for him, if it makes things easier. *(Melanie wipes her face, shakes it off.)*

MELANIE. This fear is what makes me great?

TISIPHONE. Having it — and conquering it — that's what will make you great. *(Beat.)* What I said before, about you not having the stuff? *(Melanie nods.)* You do — and then some. You're not a fourteen-year-old girl anymore, you'll do whatever you have to.

MELANIE. *(Wiping away the last of her tears.)* I *hate* that we're all splitting up …

TISIPHONE. Please, you've seen the *X-Men* movies. It's what *all* the best superhero teams do. We'll be fine. And maybe the Oracle's wrong. Or maybe Prospero … *(Ariel and Sasia rush on to another part of the stage, shielding themselves from Prospero, who strides in after them, swinging his staff viciously. Behind them: Miranda.)*

PROSPERO. SLAVES! WORTHLESS!

TISIPHONE. … Maybe he'll have a change of heart. *(Tisiphone and Melanie exit, as Prospero and his children take over the stage. We are back on the island.)*

ARIEL. PITY, Father — pity!

SASIA. Mercy, Father — MERCY! *(Prospero stops in mid-swing, his staff held aloft.)*

PROSPERO. Pity — mercy — Once, children, I had room in my heart for these, but that was — *(Raises the staff even further.)* LONG AGO!

ARIEL. Your precious Art —

PROSPERO. *Is* enchanted. Whatever you think you saw, they fooled you.

SASIA. Forgive us!

PROSPERO. FORGIVE YOU?

ARIEL. We saw him rip its pages — !

PROSPERO. Silence, Ariel — for as I sewed Miranda's mouth shut, so I will yours. *(They look towards Miranda, who turns around to face them — and the audience — fully. Indeed, Miranda's mouth has been sewn shut with needle and thread.)*

ARIEL. Believe us, Father, the boy started to rip your book apart!

PROSPERO. *(Exploding.)* ONLY A SORCERER COULD HAVE RIPPED THROUGH THE SPELL THAT PROTECTS IT! *(Pause.)* How ignorant you are of the world beyond this island, Ariel. Magic is dead in the New World. They live in a darker age than they imagine. *(Beat.)* But I will make it darker yet. Your brother believes he is beyond my reach because an ocean separates us — but I will show him how long my arms are. I will find him myself. I will atomize whoever has allied with him. And from there — finally! — I will move across the globe, towards Genoa.

SASIA. But Sycorax's curse —

PROSPERO. Demands that my feet never leave this island, yes.

(Turns to:) Miranda, go to my cell. Bring me the ax Caliban uses to chop wood. *(Miranda does not move.)* I haven't cut your tongue out yet, Daughter. You might speak again one day. *(Miranda goes.)*

ARIEL. Father ...

PROSPERO. It is a terrible price to pay, children, and I thank you for your sacrifice.

SASIA. *Our* — ?

PROSPERO. One foot — from each of you — to replace mine own pair, which I will cut off and leave here.

SASIA. You would do that, Father? Mutilate us?

ARIEL. Are you finally realizing, sister, how little we mean to him? How he would chop us to pieces, like kindling, if need be? *(Turns to Prospero.)* Isn't that so, father? *(Miranda returns with the ax, which she gives to Prospero.)*

PROSPERO. You first, Ariel. *(He raises the ax.)* Close your eyes, child. *(Blackout. The THUNK-THUNK-THUNK of an ax. The lights come up on a basement office in the bowels of Columbia University. Linda Summers, from the play's first scene, enters, followed by Melanie. She's carrying Prospero's book.)*

LINDA. Destroy it? You're actually asking *me* to destroy Prospero's book of magic?

MELANIE. *(Sheepishly.)* Can you?

LINDA. Why don't you ask me, rather, to — *shred* the Shroud of Turin?

MELANIE. *(Backtracking.)* Okay.

LINDA. Or maybe you'd like me to use the Dead Sea Scrolls for scrap paper?

MELANIE. I'm sorry.

LINDA. Or why don't I wrap my leftover Veggie Delite in the first folio of Shakespeare's plays?

MELANIE. I get it.

LINDA. Or even better, ask me to go back in time and set a match to the Library of Alexandria.

MELANIE. *(Annoyed now.)* Okay, it was a bad idea, forget I said anything. *(Linda sets the book down on a table, sits in front of it.)*

LINDA. This book is over four hundred years old. It's wrapped in human skin. No, not even — it's wrapped in magic. A chainsaw couldn't hurt it.

MELANIE. I know, that's why I was thinking that you — That maybe you could — Can you read it — decipher it?

LINDA. Of course not, look at each page. *(She opens the book to show Melanie.)* The symbols at the top are runes — runic symbols. They "lock" each page — so that it can't be read. Only magicians can unlock the runes. Unlock the runes, you can read the page. Read the page aloud, you can cast a spell. The magic is in the *words*. That's why books of magic are so valuable. Spells are notoriously difficult to memorize.

MELANIE. I'm sorry — Columbia lets you *major* in this?

LINDA. I'm — doing an independent study.

MELANIE. Do you by any chance happen to know any magicians? To unlock the runes? Any, uhm — Wiccans or, uh…?

LINDA. Even if I did, I doubt they'd be any help. Each magician has his own system, his own language.

MELANIE. That no one else knows …

LINDA. Well, it would have to be someone close to him. A wife, a father.

MELANIE. Or a — *(Realizes it as she says it.)* would a daughter know?

LINDA. Possibly. *(Her mind racing now, Melanie stands to go.)*

MELANIE. If I can even get to her … *(Melanie starts to take the book from Linda, who doesn't want to let it go.)*

LINDA. No, you don't.

MELANIE. *What?* What are you doing?

LINDA. I wanna know how you — a nothing, a nobody, a fucking dramaturg — how you got your hands on Prospero's book of magic.

MELANIE. Let — *(They struggle for the book.)* go.

LINDA. Is he alive? Have you seen him? *(A pause of disbelief: This can't be happening!)*

MELANIE. You're crazy.

LINDA. The book's not yours!

MELANIE. It's not yours either! *(Linda doesn't release.)* And I have Annie Oakley's pistol in my purse, and I'm an excellent shot, and I have nothing to lose. *(A tense moment: What's gonna happen?)*

LINDA. All right, fine. *(Linda releases the book.)*

MELANIE. You don't want to be any more involved than you already are. *(Melanie starts out.)*

LINDA. Says the rank amateur who doesn't even know what runes are. Who probably doesn't even know that the fires downtown are magical. *(This stops Melanie, who turns back to Linda.)*

MELANIE. What fires? What are you talking about?

41

LINDA. Even this far uptown, you can see them burning. An orange glow that looks … unearthly, unnatural. *Magical. (Beat.)* It's not the first time this sort of thing has happened in New York.

MELANIE. Where?

LINDA. The East Side, the teens between A and B.

MELANIE. The East — ? *(Refusing to believe it.)* Oh, God. I live on Thirteenth Street — at Thirteenth and A.

LINDA. Not anymore you don't. *(She smiles. Evilly:)* Tell me where you got the book.

MELANIE. She said she burnt my cell, that's what she meant, my apartment … *(Feeling the horror of it:)* My — life, my entire world, everything that's me … *(Anger, confusion.) Why are they doing this?*

LINDA. All right: *Don't* tell me. But earlier today? I was talking about Prospero and his book, the most powerful — *(Mini-beat.)* and now here it is. The most potent — *(Mini-beat.)* and that's *not* coincidence. There are no coincidences, there are no accidents. There's just magic, a balance to everything, which has been … tipped somehow. Very recently. I can feel it. Something's changed, something — radical.

MELANIE. *(Realizing it.)* Oh, my God … It's — him, he's — arrived.

LINDA. *(Hyperventilating.)* Prospero? Whom I've been studying all my life? He *is* alive, then, he's here?! Tell me where! Or let me come with you! I can help!

MELANIE. I don't think so. Only one person can — *maybe* — if she's even alive still … *(She clutches Prospero's book tightly — and rushes out. Linda looks after Melanie, then follows her out — as the lights shift to another part of the stage, where Chet stands, the master of all he surveys.)*

CHET. Gravesend. The part of Coney Island no one comes to anymore, past the lights and the rides and the wooden planks. The end of the island. No houses, just … empty lots. Rocky water. This was the first place I thought of to hide you, Caliban. By the ocean's edge, so that if the heat gets too much for you, you could — *(Short pause.)* Caliban? *(He looks around, but nobody's there.)* You were right behind me, we took the subway, I called Tisiphone to meet us here, and then — *(Beat.)* Oh, shit. Oh, shit, did I lose you? Are you lost? *(From the shadows of Coney Island, a low, ominous voice calls out to Chet.)*

CALIBAN'S VOICE. Chester …

CHET. Caliban? *(Relief.)* I thought you were ditching me.

CALIBAN'S VOICE. Succulent, succulent Chester …

CHET. Caliban? What are you talk — ? (*Caliban steps from the shadows. He is much, MUCH more reptilian now. Greenish skin, hunched over, more pronounced fins running down his back, even a tail-like growth. Webbed feet now, too. Chet starts backing away from him.*) Oh my God. An hour ago you were —

CALIBAN. You see mine own true self revealed …

CHET. It's okay, we can fix this, we can —

CALIBAN. Do not be afeared …

CHET. Oh, I'm not, I'm just — (*Realizing it.*) Oh, gross, Caliban, you're *drooling.*

CALIBAN. I'm so hungry, Chester, for …

CHET. A hot dog? There's a Nathan's just down the boardwalk, not far —

CALIBAN. Warm blood … Human flesh … (*Chet stops backing away, bravely tries to reason with him.*)

CHET. This isn't you, Caliban, it's your father's magic causing you to —

CALIBAN. (*Still advancing.*) I am a devil, a born devil … on whose nature nurture can never stick … (*Chet holds up his orange life-preserver thing as a weapon.*)

CHET. Don't make me hurt you, Caliban.

CALIBAN. You are the sweetest meat, Chester …

CHET. (*Trying a different tactic.*) Think of Miranda!

CALIBAN. I'll have her, too, and people this island with Calibans …

CHET. Oh, God — (*Caliban is almost upon Chet, who raises the preserver to strike in self-defense. Tisiphone enters, dressed like a secret agent, brandishing a small, fashionable dart gun. She raises it, pointing it towards Chet and Caliban.*)

TISIPHONE. Go down, Chet!

CHET. What?

TISIPHONE. Duck, fool! (*Chet does, and Tisiphone fires over him, hitting Caliban in the chest with a small dart. Caliban plucks it out and almost immediately starts swaying drunkenly. Pleased with herself.*) Just call me Pussy Galore.

CALIBAN. Wh … what?

TISIPHONE. Beneath our neocortexes and our limbic systems, Caliban, are our reptile brains, which control our aggressions and appetites. It's what your father, I'm betting, shifted into overdrive with his magic. (*Caliban pitches forward, unconscious, and Chet catches him, barely able to support the weight.*)

CHET. It's okay, I got him, I got him — *(He drops Caliban.)* *Whoops …*

TISIPHONE. Thing is: Appetites can be suppressed with science, with chemicals. Like on the tip of that dart. I have friends in pharmaceuticals — that's where I was, seeing them — and they whipped me up a batch of … let's call them "appetite suppressants." *(Tisiphone steps in closer for a gander.)* And looky-looky: It's already working. The scales on his hands —

CHET. — They're dissolving.

TISIPHONE. Magic, science, it's all the same, sweetheart.

CHET. So he's gonna be okay, then? Caliban, I mean?

TISIPHONE. He's gonna be human — as human as he was. *(Tisiphone starts to shimmy and shake. She pulls a cell phone from her cleavage, turns to Chet.)* Had it on vibrate. *(Answers.)* All hail! Melanie, Pussycat, I was just about to ask Encyclopedia Brown if he'd called you. *(Beat.)* I'm fine. *(Beat.)* Chet's fine. *(Winks at Chet, looks down at Caliban.)* Caliban's — getting there. Slow down, you sound — Hold on, something's wrong with my reception. You're cutting in and out, and I'm hearing what sounds suspiciously like — *(Tisiphone moves away from Chet and Caliban. As she does that, Melanie walks on from the other side of the stage. The lights shift and crossfade, narrowing on Melanie. As she enters and takes over the stage, Melanie has her cell phone in one hand and Annie Oakley's revolver in the other, raised, pointing, and — BANG! BANG! BANG! Shooting at something, seen or unseen. Once she is alone on stage, Melanie lowers the gun and we hear her half of the conversation.)*

MELANIE. — Gunshots? That was me, Tisiphone, I just — oh, God! — I just shot the Mad Hatter! *(Beat.)* No, from the Alice in Wonderland statues in Central Park — that's where I am! It came to life and it — it came at me! And not just *his* statue, all over the city! The lions in front of the library, those enormous stone lions! Tearing through Grand Central! The entire city's changing, Tisiphone — coming to life — coming apart! *(Beat.)* That's what I'm trying to tell you: Prospero's here already — he must be. *(Beat.)* No, first I have to — *(Beat.)* No, I know where that is, by the water; wait for me, stay hidden. *(Significantly.)* And don't let anything happen to Chet. *(Melanie hangs up. She reaches into her bag and pulls out the Arden edition of* The Tempest. *Kneeling down:)* My magic can't just be about setting characters free from plays. It's the principle — the summoning — that counts. *(She presses the halves of the book down, concentrates.*) Come on, I can *feel* you inside there, the real Miranda, buried beneath this play. I can feel the tips of my fingers brushing up against your hair, your … *(She tries again.)* Let my mind clear. Let the words fall away. Let the pages float off the spine. And open … the … door. And … Watch … it … swing … open? *(Melanie stops, listens attentively. Finally, after a long, disheartening silence, we hear it: the telltale bell. Melanie turns to see: Miranda, taking tentative steps from the dark, pulling the thread from her mouth as she moves into the light.)* Oh my God. *(Horrified.)* What's he done to you?

MIRANDA. Where on Earth — ? Why have you — *(She pulls the last of the thread out.)* Why have you brought me here?

MELANIE. *(Quoting* The Tempest.*)* "Admired Miranda, worth what's dearest to the world."

MIRANDA. What are you — a witch? *(Miranda gasps.)* Yes! The raven-haired maiden, with owl eyes!

MELANIE. *(Conceding finally.)* — yes.

MIRANDA. You have Father's book …

MELANIE. Caliban found me, yes, and he — *(Melanie picks up Prospero's book, clutches it.)* Caliban told me you helped him escape the island, that you set him free even though his chains were magic, is that right? *(Miranda nods.)* How did you unlock the spell that held them together?

MIRANDA. Carved into the metal were runic symbols of my father's invention. My father had a custom that he would sleep in the afternoons. During those quiet hours, I would study his books and scrolls. Slowly, over years, I taught myself the language of his runes. *(Melanie kneels down in front of Miranda. She opens up Prospero's book.)*

MELANIE. Show me. *(Miranda looks the runes over, nods.)*

MIRANDA. But after I open the cage, who will tame what lives inside it? Only a magician of immense power would be able to —

MELANIE. Me. *(Beat.)* I will. *(Miranda nods her head, and the lights shift — as the girls exit — to: The Statue of Liberty's torch. Ariel and Sasia stand looking out over the city. The wind whips around them. Sasia peers intently into the night.)*

ARIEL. Foul weather, Sister.

SASIA. Very foul, indeed.

ARIEL. From this height, we can fairly touch the sky … *(He looks up, into the menacing, swirling clouds.)* Look, Sasia, how it changes colors with Father's moods. Red, for his fury. Purple, for his wounded pride. Yellow, for his fear.

SASIA. His fear, Brother?

ARIEL. Can't you see it on him? Or smell it? It sits on his shoulders like a coat.

SASIA. Caliban will be stopped. His allies will be crushed.

ARIEL. Assuredly. Without question. We'll see to it. *(Pause.)* Unless …

SASIA. *(Searching the horizon.)* Where *are* they?

ARIEL. Could *we* not take the island for ourselves? *(For the first time in this scene, Sasia pauses in her search, straightens up. Ariel continues, brimming with hatred.)* He uses us like mules, like shields — and when we're damaged beyond repair, he'll cast us off. Would he ever do to Caliban what he's done to us?

SASIA. Brother, do not —

ARIEL. *Our feet, Sister. (Short pause.)* He feels Caliban's betrayal most acutely because he loves him most. Caliban and Miranda, his oldest and his youngest, his most precious. *(Beat.)* Father's fury towards Caliban will pass — but now it burns white-hot and blinds him to all other threats.

SASIA. We would be as mice trying to fell an elephant.

ARIEL. Father will *never* free us, Sasia, we are slaves. *(Beat.)* I cannot do it alone.

SASIA. Ah, then it cannot be done. *(Before Ariel is able to protest again.)* Hold your tongue, Brother, I *smell* him. *(Indeed, Prospero enters, his black cloak billowing around him.)*

ARIEL. *(Still looking at Sasia.)* How were your travels, father?

PROSPERO. Devoid of magic though it be, this New World fairly teems with marvels. What country, Ariel, is this?

ARIEL. It is called … New York, father.

PROSPERO. And this we stand on?

ARIEL. The Statue of Liberty, Father.

PROSPERO. Is that what they build monuments to in the New World — liberty?

ARIEL. From this vantage, we may gaze out across the entire city — and, in a single moment, drink in our labors. *(Prospero turns to Sasia.)*

PROSPERO. All rests on you now, my huntress. I gave you a hawk's eyes, a perch high above this starry kingdom. Do not disappoint me, Daughter. Precious as your foot was, I've no doubt your hands —

SASIA. *(Finally! Success!)* I see them, Father!

PROSPERO. All of them?

SASIA. Brother Caliban and — yes, others, too. A woman, an

Amazon by her looks, and a boy.

PROSPERO. The child-warrior?

SASIA. Yes, Father. Carrying … a spearhead of destiny? Can that be?

ARIEL. Has the fourth been here all along? In the New World?

PROSPERO. And the raven-haired maiden, Sasia?

SASIA. No, Father.

PROSPERO. Has she abandoned them, I wonder? *(To Sasia.)* Well done, my tricksy spirit! Affix them with your eyes, daughter, and lead us to them. Let the night air carry us down. *(Prospero raises his arms, his cloak billows around them, and then he, Ariel, and Sasia are gone. The lights shift to Gravesend. The end of the boardwalk. Caliban, back to his old self, Tisiphone, and Chet are there. Chet is looking up into the sky.)*

CHET. Uhm, guys? What's happening to the sky? All the colors? *(Looks around some more.)* And that sound? What's that noise?

CALIBAN. Which sound?

CHET. And the air? Doesn't it feel all, like, weird?

TISIPHONE. The eve of Orestes' trial, held at Apollo's temple, the sky was like this one — the color of blood, and vengeance, and destruction. The air was choked with portents of violence and death.

CHET. *(Cocking his head suddenly.)* There it is again, I can't believe you guys don't hear that, it's like wings flapping … *(Caliban stops, takes a step away from Chet. His eyes widen in horror.)* What? What is it?

CALIBAN. The wings you hear … The Angel of Death circling you like a vulture …

CHET. *(Scared, maybe for the first time in the play.)* What? *(Shakes his head.)* No way, you're — you're crazy.

CALIBAN. *(Quickly.)* Chester — Tisiphone — take my hands. *(They do.)* Now and forever, you are my brothers. Your bravery honors you both. And I — *(He kneels down.)* — I honor you both. You had no cause to join me, yet you have willingly faced forces that would set lesser men to hide behind their mothers' skirts. The blast of war blows in your ears, and you imitate the action of tigers. You stiffen your sinews, you summon up your blood, you disguise your fair nature with hard-favour'd rage, and you lend your eyes a terrible aspect. *(Caliban stands.)* If any of us should fall tonight, whoever survives — whoever lives — will carry our departed's spirit with them forever. I pledge this.

TISIPHONE. So do I.

CHET. Me, too. *(The sound of hollow applause. Prospero enters, clapping.)*

PROSPERO. What a fine General you've become, my son.

CALIBAN. *(Breaking away from the circle.)* Father —

PROSPERO. I would follow you into battle. My sword raised, my shield shouldered.

CALIBAN. Sycorax's curse — ?

PROSPERO. Sacrifices have been made. *(He lifts up his robes, revealing black thread where new feet have been sewn to the stumps. He calls over his shoulder:)* Sasia, Ariel! *(They enter, and we now see clearly that each of them is missing a foot.)*

CHET. Oh my gosh.

CALIBAN. *(Almost to himself.)* Hell is empty and all the devils are here …

TISIPHONE. Stay right next to me, Chet. No matter what happens.

PROSPERO. Come, children, and see how mine enemies are at my mercy. *(Turns back.)* Caliban, for your betrayal, your torments should be unending. And yet … Your resourcefulness and courage bear noting. End this madness now. Return me mine Art, stand by my side, and you will ascend in my favor as a firstborn should. You will sit in a station above your brother and sister. They will serve you as they serve me. *(Grabs the hair on the back of Ariel's head.)* Isn't that so?

ARIEL. Yes, Father.

PROSPERO. *(To Caliban as he releases Ariel.)* Also: I will teach you to read and write. I will give you the secrets of my Art. I will radiate mine every affection on you like a sun. *(Short pause.)* I will even, if you like, appoint you Miranda's keeper, so you might satisfy whatever appetites you would with her — *(Caliban spits in Prospero's face.)* Or I will hack you and your friends into messes.

CALIBAN. Your book isn't here, Father. And if you kill any of us, you'll never find it.

PROSPERO. If need be, I will turn this city and its people to ash. I have already begun to do so. How much would you sacrifice, Caliban?

CALIBAN. Not hope, which I clutch onto so long as I have breath.

PROSPERO. I think I'll start with … *(His eyes fall on Chet.)* You, whelp.

CHET. Me?

PROSPERO. Sasia, Ariel — tear him limb from limb. *(Sasia and Ariel stalk towards Chet, who pulls out the Spear of Destiny. This stops them momentarily.)*

CHET. Just try it.

TISIPHONE. You see? We have teeth, too.

CHET. *(Cocky — too cocky.)* It's called the Spear of Destiny, ever heard of it?

ARIEL. More than heard, pup. *(He pulls a spear from his belt. It looks exactly like the Spear of Destiny.)* But yours is one of two. *(Sasia pulls a spear from her belt. Again, it's exactly like Chet's.)*

SASIA. Of three. *(Ariel pulls out another spear.)*

ARIEL. Of four.

PROSPERO. The spearheads aren't magic, whelp, they *channel* magic — the magic and will of whoever wields it. You may be a warrior, but you're not magical. *(Turns to:)* When you're done with him, Ariel, I want his head impaled on a lance. *(Caliban and Tisiphone move to intercept Ariel and Sasia. Before they meet, however, we hear the sudden, terrifying sound of thunder. Everyone stops.)*

ARIEL. Father?

SASIA. Is that your thunder? *(More thunder. Then another sound. Tisiphone holds up a cupped hand. She looks up into the sky.)*

TISIPHONE. What — ? *(Chet opens his arms wide. He is almost laughing.)*

CHET. Holy shit, it's raining! Cold — freezing — rain! *(Indeed, the sound we are hearing is raindrops. Big, fat, wonderful summer raindrops.)*

TISIPHONE. Not just rain, cupcake —

CALIBAN. Enchanted rain. Called down by magic. *(Realizing it.)* The raven-haired maiden!

PROSPERO. *(A touch of panic, perhaps?)* What? *(Melanie slowly walks in, holding Prospero's book open before her. Miranda follows her on.)*

MELANIE. The thing about magic is: You mustn't try to control it. You must — surrender to it. Open yourself to it. *(She fixes Prospero with a gaze.)* I did, and once Miranda had unlocked your runes for me —

PROSPERO. *You,* daughter?

MIRANDA. I begged you to stop, Father.

MELANIE. — Once Miranda had done that, the letters in your book swirled around like alphabet soup and I *could* read your spells — like the one that calls down rain — to put out, finally, the fires your children started.

PROSPERO. Ariel, forget the pup. This woman first. *(Ariel moves towards Melanie, who very calmly turns to another page in Prospero's book. She reads:)*

49

MELANIE. "Pour down, yellow sun, and thicken air to amber; Snare foul foe in harden'd chamber." *(A yellow light strikes Ariel in mid-stride, as he slows to a halt as though his blood were solidifying.)*

ARIEL. You — wench — what … have … you … *(But Ariel is still, completely motionless, like a statue.)*

PROSPERO. Sasia!

SASIA. I half-burned you before, lady, this time — *(Melanie turns to another page of Prospero's book. She reads:)*

MELANIE. "A winter season visits this year twice, Transforming heat of fiery hell to crystall'd ice." *(A blue light strikes Sasia, who starts to shake uncontrollably, as though the blood in her veins were freezing solid.)*

SASIA. F-f-f-father? What has she … *(But Sasia is frozen solid, like a block of ice. Melanie, meantime, starts flipping the pages in Prospero's book. She turns to him.)*

MELANIE. I found one in here that's *perfect* for you …

PROSPERO. That is quite enough. *(Prospero claps his hands, and the book Melanie is holding snaps shut.)*

CHET. Melanie — ?

MELANIE. *(As she struggles with the book.)* I can't — It won't open. *(Turns to:)* Tisiphone?

TISIPHONE. Way ahead of you. *(Tisiphone pulls out her sword and advances on Prospero, who turns to her.)*

PROSPERO. You — Fury — it is beyond even *my* power to hurt you —

TISIPHONE. I know.

PROSPERO. — But a binding spell ensures you return the kindness *(A cone of white light from above strikes Tisiphone, trapping her where she stands.)*

TISIPHONE. Melanie, I can't —

PROSPERO. *(Holding out a hand.)* Deliver me my Art. *(Caliban snatches the book from Melanie.)*

CALIBAN. Not until they've left this place. Let them go, father. I'll stay behind, but let them go free.

PROSPERO. This grows tiresome. My Art — to me — *NOW.* *(Caliban, unable to help himself, like a puppet, goes to Prospero, delivers the book.)* You are a fish, you cannot breathe. *(Caliban's eyes widen. He starts gasping and falls down. Miranda rushes to Caliban as Melanie moves towards Prospero.)* And so they all fall like pins, and nothing stands between the wicked sorcerer and his darker purpose but — *(He turns to Melanie.)* You, raven-haired maiden. Destined to become the greatest sorcerer of all time, and yet … Where is *your* book of magic? Your *Art?*

CHET. Mel — "darker purpose" — that's from *King Lear* —

MELANIE. Get out of here, Chet!

PROSPERO. All these years — for centuries — I've lived in fear, and here you are before me: defenseless.

CHET. You *do* have a magic book.

MELANIE. Chet — !

CHET. Your magic, Mel, not his. *(But Melanie is making eye contact with Miranda.)*

MELANIE. Now, Miranda! *(Prospero turns to face Miranda, who throws a handful of sand into his face.)*

MIRANDA. Sand from my mother's island to blind you! *(Prospero shrieks as the sand hits eyes and he is momentarily blinded.)*

MELANIE. Good, Miranda, now go — both of you! I'll hold him as long as I can!

CHET. Use *King Lear,* Mel!

MELANIE. How, Chet? Who in *King Lear* could stop Prospero? Who's powerful enough to — ? *(Realizes something.)* Oh, God. Not who — what. *(Melanie clambers to her purse, starts going through it.)*

TISIPHONE. Whatever you're thinking, Pussy Cat, do it faster — faster! *(Melanie pulls the Arden edition of* King Lear *from her purse and holds it open with the palms of her hands. She closes her eyes, concentrates — just as Prospero rubs the last of the sand from his eyes.)*

PROSPERO. And still you hope. Remarkable …

MELANIE. Come on, come on … like … opening … a … door …

PROSPERO. Sycorax destroyed the Book of Destiny's last page. Did she know how this story would end? *(He holds up both of his hands and clenches them into fists.)* With my Art slowing your heart's beating to *nothing,* drying the blood in your veins to *powder,* hardening the air in your lungs to — *(All this is happening to Melanie; her entire body arcs in pain. But Chet has circled around Prospero; he stabs him in the back with the spear! Prospero howls with pain — his spell on Melanie breaks! — and the magician wheels on Chet, pulling the spear from his back.)* You — child-warrior! *(Prospero snaps his fingers and a pomegranate appears in his right hand.)* This is your best part, whelp: Your heart. *(With the spear, Prospero punctures the pomegranate. Blood seeps from the fruit, and … Chet is in agony! Grasping his chest as he slips to the ground, convulsing. Miranda goes to Chet, puts her hand on his chest.)*

MIRANDA. *(To Melanie.)* His heart — beating so fast it will burst!

MELANIE. Chet! Are you — ?

CHET. … Keep going …

PROSPERO. *(Looking down at Chet.)* All this time you were chasing after your destiny, unaware that *it* had been pursuing *you*. What a pity your sacrifice gains you nothing. *(Prospero turns to Melanie, who has returned to her task.* King Lear *is open before her. She is completing the spell.)*

MELANIE. Like … opening … a … door? *(Melanie looks up expectantly. She strains to hear it. And finally we all do: the little bell signaling a door opening somewhere. Then:)*

PROSPERO. A summoning? What have you called forth, maiden? *(Melanie stands, reading an excerpt from* King Lear:*)*

MELANIE.
Blow, winds, and crack your cheeks!
Rage! Blow!
You cataracts and hurricanoes, spout
Till you have drench'd our steeples!

TISIPHONE. A storm? You set the storm on the heath free?

MELANIE. *(Still reading.)*
The body's delicate: the tempest in my mind
Doth from my senses take all feeling else
Save what beats there.

PROSPERO. What is a storm without lightning? Without wind howl — *(Something catches in Prospero's throat.)* Without it — *(And again.)* howl … ing …

MELANIE. Not on the heath, Tisiphone, the storm in Lear's mind …

PROSPERO. Howl …

TISIPHONE. You set Lear's madness free?

PROSPERO. Howl …

MELANIE. And transplanted it. *(Prospero drops his book like a dead weight. Slowly, his hands move to his head, which he grips ferociously.)*

PROSPERO. *(Gone mad.)* Howl … Howl … *(Prospero looks closely at Melanie, at Tisiphone.)* Who are you? *(Waves his hand in front of Tisiphone, breaking the binding spell.)* Mine eyes are not o' the best: I'll tell you straight.

TISIPHONE. Gods. Lear's madness in Prospero's head.

MELANIE. Chet was right — my magic … *(Prospero approaches Caliban, kneels next to him.)*

PROSPERO. No — no — no life? Why should a dog, a horse, a rat, have life, and thou no breath at all?

MIRANDA. Save him — make it right! *(Prospero touches Caliban's forehead.)*

PROSPERO. Breathe easy, fool. *(With that, Caliban's breathing does become regular — evens out. Prospero stands again. Miranda goes to Chet's body, lifts it up towards her father.)*

MIRANDA. This one! You save this boy, too!

PROSPERO. *(Shaking his head.)*
Never, never, never, never, never …
Once, I might have saved him, now …
Never …
Never …
Never …
Never …

(Prospero is wandering away now, lost in a cloud of madness. Chet coughs — there is still some life in him!)

CHET. Mel-lanie …

TISIPHONE. *(Meaning Prospero.)* We have to follow him, we can't just let him — *(Prospero is gone. Melanie kneels next to Chet.)*

MELANIE. He doesn't know who he is, who we are, what he wants — let him vanish. *(Looks down at the child-warrior.)* I'm here, Chet, I'm holding your hand. *(Caliban sits up, grabbing his chest.)*

CALIBAN. La-lady …

CHET. *(To Melanie.)* Did we — did we — ?

MELANIE. Yes, Chet, we did it, we stopped him. We're all safe — we're all saved.

CHET. So you — you really are —

MELANIE. Don't talk, Chet. *(Chet coughs, convulses. He's barely alive. Caliban approaches him.)*

CALIBAN. Child-warrior …

CHET. W-who?

MELANIE. It's Caliban, Chet, can't you see him?

CHET. I'm not — scared …

TISIPHONE. Of course you're not, baby.

CALIBAN. *(To Chet.)* Take this knowledge with you into Elysium. That my father is vanquished — my mother's island is restored — and this New World is preserved — because of you.

CHET. *(Gasping.)* Oh — God — Mel — ? *(Chet is leaving this world. Melanie is crying.)*

53

MELANIE. Close your eyes, Chet. *(She does it for him.)* Do you see them? All along the highlands, in the mist, your ancestors ... raising their shields for you — honoring you — welcoming you ... *(Her heart breaks.)* Oh, God ... *(The lights slowly fade on our heroes until all that's left is blackness, the night sky, filled with rain and clouds and the stars of a new constellation: a young man, a boy really. The night sky shrinks until it is only a window in a padded cell in Bellevue Psychiatric Hospital. Prospero is there, cowed, restrained in a straitjacket. Linda Summers is standing nearby. She takes a step towards Prospero just as Dr. Rosemary Ridgeon enters brusquely.)*

RIDGEON. Sorry to keep you waiting, Ms. Summers. Ever since the fires, most of Bellevue's staff has been working round-the-clock at St. Vincent's. We're on a skeleton crew here, I'm afraid.

LINDA. Must you restrain him that way? Like an animal?

RIDGEON. I'm afraid so. He — went berserk right before his MRI. Broke one orderly's jaw, clawed another one's face open. He's on the fourteenth floor, in surgery. The orderly, I mean. They're trying to save his eyes.

LINDA. Did the MRI show anything?

RIDGEON. There are lesions covering almost ninety percent of his brain. The kind commonly associated with Alzheimer's or Lewey's Dementia, which is what I think we're dealing with here.

LINDA. Lewey's Dementia. But that's ... incurable.

RIDGEON. Right now it is, but perhaps in time ... *(Beat.)* For the present, though, we can burn the lesions off, keep him sedated. We can ease his suffering, at least. That's something.

LINDA. *(Looking at Prospero.)* How tragic. So ... Shakespearean.

RIDGEON. You very likely saved this man's life, Ms. Summers. Most New Yorkers happen across someone like him, they look the other way. Very few would do what you did: Deliver him to us, pay for his treatment.

LINDA. I consider it an investment in my future, Doctor.

RIDGEON. Sorry? *(She suddenly reaches into her coat, pulls out her pager.)* Bloody hell, I should finish my rounds. Will you be all right here?

LINDA. Look at him, Doctor — of course I will be. *(Ridgeon nods, exits. Linda takes a step towards Prospero.)* I didn't "happen" across you. I followed that woman from my office, across the city. I ... saw what she and her friends did to you. How they ... humiliated you. It was over so quickly, I couldn't help you then, but ... I *can* help you now. I'll bring you back from wherever you are, I promise. And then … you can teach me your magic, yes? *(Beat.)* Do you understand any of what I'm saying? Wherever you are, Prospero, you are *not* alone … *(The lights fade on the scene until only Prospero's face remains. Eventually that light goes out, as well, and we cross-fade to: Prospero's island. The beach. An idyllic scene. Caliban and Miranda are playing chess. Tisiphone, looking fabulous in a bikini, sits on a lounger, sipping a frozen margarita. Melanie, dressed for the beach in a sarong, is staring out across the ocean — across the audience. She holds Prospero's book close to her heart.)*

MELANIE. *(To the audience.)* Even now, Prospero's face still surfaces sometimes — unbidden, darkening my dreams, after all these …

Well, time moves differently here on this enchanted island, doesn't it? Seconds are minutes are hours are years are blinks of an eye …

At dawn, kingdoms are born, and by sundown, entire civilizations are crumbled … (That's what it feels like, anyway.)

It is a wondrous place, unchanged, frozen in time, since Sycorax's curse. Until now, when every day brings new delights, and more of its former glory returns.

Its beauty makes our sacrifices easier, somehow. *(Beat.)* No, it doesn't.

There is a beach, on the other side of the island, a narrow strip of yellow sand, surrounded by the bluest water, as far as the eye can see, where I have buried our dead: Mr. Shylock, Caius Marcius, the people who burned in the fires that terrible night, and … Chet.

I visit their graves each morning. *(Short pause.)* I don't know how long I'll stay here, beautiful as it is, I'm a New York City girl, but … there are advantages.

There is a library like no other, with volumes and volumes of —

I have time to read, to study. And every day, I unlock another page, another two pages, another four pages, of a volume that seems endless because, perhaps, it is.

There is one spell in particular I'm looking for. I don't know for certain that it exists, but I think it does.

I — pray it does.

There's a quote from *The Tempest* that fills me with hope, and it is this: "By my so potent Art, with Jove's own bolt, graves at my command have opened and waked their sleepers."

I'm looking for that spell. Maybe Shakespeare made it up, but I don't think so.

A spell to bring them back to life, those who gave so much. *(Melanie keeps looking out at the ocean as the lights on the stage start to go out, go out, go out … are gone.)*

End of Play

PROPERTY LIST

Projection of Henry Fuseli's painting *The Tempest*
Walking staff
Manacles and chains
Orange life-preserver
Frozen margaritas (3)
Napkin
Whistle
Purse with money
Purple flower
2 sheets of parchment
Cordless phone
Mail
2 enormous ancient books
Bell on bookstore's counter
Copies of *The Tempest, King Lear,* and *Coriolanus* (Arden editions, if possible)
Picture of Ariel
Piece of paper
Plates and silverware
Plastic see-through umbrellas
Wigs with "writhing snakes"
Large Bloomingdale's bag
Bloody severed head
Umbrella with 2 swords hidden in the handle
A flare (torch)
Cell phones
Old-fashioned pistol
Several rocky ancient-looking spears
Ax
Several regular spear heads
Dart gun and darts
Handful of sand
Pomegranate with dripping blood
Pager
Beach lounger
Chess board

SOUND EFFECTS

Thunderclaps
Sounds of a hurricane
Sound of a ship breaking apart
Snappy, fun music
Knock on door
Little bell ringing
Fire engines
Disco music
Ax chopping
Gunshots
A punch in the jaw
Rain

NEW PLAYS

★ **MOTHERS AND SONS by Terrence McNally.** At turns funny and powerful, MOTHERS AND SONS portrays a woman who pays an unexpected visit to the New York apartment of her late son's partner, who is now married to another man and has a young son. Challenged to face how society has changed around her, generations collide as she revisits the past and begins to see the life her son might have led. "A resonant elegy for a ravaged generation." –NY Times. "A moving reflection on a changed America." –Chicago Tribune. [2M, 1W, 1 boy] ISBN: 978-0-8222-3183-7

★ **THE HEIR APPARENT by David Ives, adapted from Le Légataire Universel by Jean-François Regnard.** Paris, 1708. Eraste, a worthy though penniless young man, is in love with the fair Isabelle, but her forbidding mother, Madame Argante, will only let the two marry if Eraste can show he will inherit the estate of his rich but miserly Uncle Geronte. Unfortunately, old Geronte has also fallen for the fair Isabelle, and plans to marry her this very day and leave her everything in his will—separating the two young lovers forever. Eraste's wily servant Crispin jumps in, getting a couple of meddling relatives disinherited by impersonating them (one, a brash American, the other a French female country cousin)—only to have the old man kick off before his will is made! In a brilliant stroke, Crispin then impersonates the old man, dictating a will favorable to his master (and Crispin himself, of course)—only to find that rich Uncle Geronte isn't dead at all and is more than ever ready to marry Isabelle! The multiple strands of the plot are unraveled to great comic effect in the streaming rhyming couplets of French classical comedy, and everyone lives happily, and richly, ever after. [4M, 3W] ISBN: 978-0-8222-2808-0

★ **HANDLE WITH CARE by Jason Odell Williams.** Circumstances both hilarious and tragic bring together a young Israeli woman, who has little command of English, and a young American man, who has little command of romance. Is their inevitable love an accident…or is it destiny, generations in the making? "A hilarious and heart-warming romantic comedy." –NY Times. "Hilariously funny! Utterly charming, fearlessly adorable and a tiny bit magical." –Naples News. [2M, 2W] ISBN: 978-0-8222-3138-7

★ **LAST GAS by John Cariani.** Nat Paradis is a Red Sox-loving part-time dad who manages Paradis' Last Convenient Store, the last convenient place to get gas—or anything—before the Canadian border to the north and the North Maine Woods to the west. When an old flame returns to town, Nat gets a chance to rekindle a romance he gave up on years ago. But sparks fly as he's forced to choose between new love and old. "Peppered with poignant characters [and] sharp writing." –Portland Phoenix. "Very funny and surprisingly thought-provoking." –Portland Press Herald. [4M, 3W] ISBN: 978-0-8222-3232-2

DRAMATISTS PLAY SERVICE, INC.
440 Park Avenue South, New York, NY 10016 212-683-8960 Fax 212-213-1539
postmaster@dramatists.com www.dramatists.com

NEW PLAYS

★ **ACT ONE by James Lapine.** Growing up in an impoverished Bronx family and forced to drop out of school at age thirteen, Moss Hart dreamed of joining the glamorous world of the theater. Hart's famous memoir *Act One* plots his unlikely collaboration with the legendary playwright George S. Kaufman and his arrival on Broadway. Tony Award-winning writer and director James Lapine has adapted Act One for the stage, creating a funny, heartbreaking and suspenseful celebration of a playwright and his work. "…brims contagiously with the ineffable, irrational and irrefutable passion for that endangered religion called the Theater." –NY Times. "…wrought with abundant skill and empathy." –Time Out. [8M, 4W] ISBN: 978-0-8222-3217-9

★ **THE VEIL by Conor McPherson.** May 1822, rural Ireland. The defrocked Reverend Berkeley arrives at the crumbling former glory of Mount Prospect House to accompany a young woman to England. Seventeen-year-old Hannah is to be married off to a marquis in order to resolve the debts of her mother's estate. However, compelled by the strange voices that haunt his beautiful young charge and a fascination with the psychic current that pervades the house, Berkeley proposes a séance, the consequences of which are catastrophic. "…an effective mixture of dark comedy and suspense." –Telegraph (London). "A cracking fireside tale of haunting and decay." –Times (London). [3M, 5W] ISBN: 978-0-8222-3313-8

★ **AN OCTOROON by Branden Jacobs-Jenkins. Winner of the 2014 OBIE Award for Best New American Play.** Judge Peyton is dead and his plantation Terrebonne is in financial ruins. Peyton's handsome nephew George arrives as heir apparent and quickly falls in love with Zoe, a beautiful octoroon. But the evil overseer M'Closky has other plans—for both Terrebonne and Zoe. In 1859, a famous Irishman wrote this play about slavery in America. Now an American tries to write his own. "AN OCTOROON invites us to laugh loudly and easily at how naïve the old stereotypes now seem, until nothing seems funny at all." –NY Times [10M, 5W] ISBN: 978-0-8222-3226-1

★ **IVANOV translated and adapted by Curt Columbus.** In this fascinating early work by Anton Chekhov, we see the union of humor and pathos that would become his trademark. A restless man, Nicholai Ivanov struggles to dig himself out of debt and out of provincial boredom. When the local doctor, Lvov, informs Ivanov that his wife Anna is dying and accuses him of worsening her condition with his foul moods, Ivanov is sent into a downward spiral of depression and ennui. He soon finds himself drawn to a beautiful young woman, Sasha, full of hope and energy. Finding himself stuck between a romantic young mistress and his ailing wife, Ivanov falls deeper into crisis, heading toward inevitable tragedy. [8M, 8W] ISBN: 978-0-8222-3155-4

DRAMATISTS PLAY SERVICE, INC.
440 Park Avenue South, New York, NY 10016 212-683-8960 Fax 212-213-1539
postmaster@dramatists.com www.dramatists.com

NEW PLAYS

★ **I'LL EAT YOU LAST: A CHAT WITH SUE MENGERS by John Logan.** For more than 20 years, Sue Mengers' clients were the biggest names in show business: Barbra Streisand, Faye Dunaway, Burt Reynolds, Ali MacGraw, Gene Hackman, Cher, Candice Bergen, Ryan O'Neal, Nick Nolte, Mike Nichols, Gore Vidal, Bob Fosse…If her clients were the talk of the town, she was the town, and her dinner parties were the envy of Hollywood. Now, you're invited into her glamorous Beverly Hills home for an evening of dish, dirty secrets and all the inside showbiz details only Sue can tell you. "A delectable soufflé of a solo show…thanks to the buoyant, witty writing of Mr. Logan" –NY Times. "80 irresistible minutes of primo tinseltown dish from a certified master chef." –Hollywood Reporter. [1W] ISBN: 978-0-8222-3079-3

★ **PUNK ROCK by Simon Stephens.** In a private school outside of Manchester, England, a group of highly-articulate seventeen-year-olds flirt and posture their way through the day while preparing for their A-Level mock exams. With hormones raging and minimal adult supervision, the students must prepare for their future — and survive the savagery of high school. Inspired by playwright Simon Stephens' own experiences as a teacher, PUNK ROCK is an honest and unnerving chronicle of contemporary adolescence. "[A] tender, ferocious and frightning play." –NY Times. "[A] muscular little play that starts out funny and ferocious then reveals its compassion by degrees." –Hollywood Reporter. [5M, 3W] ISBN: 978-0-8222-3288-9

★ **THE COUNTRY HOUSE by Donald Margulies.** A brood of famous and longing-to-be-famous creative artists have gathered at their summer home during the Williamstown Theatre Festival. When the weekend takes an unexpected turn, everyone is forced to improvise, inciting a series of simmering jealousies, romantic outbursts, and passionate soul-searching. Both witty and compelling, THE COUNTRY HOUSE provides a piercing look at a family of performers coming to terms with the roles they play in each other's lives. "A valentine to the artists of the stage." –NY Times. "Remarkably candid and funny." –Variety. [3M, 3W] ISBN: 978-0-8222-3274-2

★ **OUR LADY OF KIBEHO by Katori Hall.** Based on real events, OUR LADY OF KIBEHO is an exploration of faith, doubt, and the power and consequences of both. In 1981, a village girl in Rwanda claims to see the Virgin Mary. Ostracized by her schoolmates and labeled disturbed, everyone refuses to believe, until impossible happenings appear again and again. Skepticism gives way to fear, and then to belief, causing upheaval in the school community and beyond. "Transfixing." –NY Times. "Hall's passionate play renews belief in what theater can do." –Time Out [7M, 8W, 1 boy] ISBN: 978-0-8222-3301-5

DRAMATISTS PLAY SERVICE, INC.
440 Park Avenue South, New York, NY 10016 212-683-8960 Fax 212-213-1539
postmaster@dramatists.com www.dramatists.com

NEW PLAYS

★ **AGES OF THE MOON by Sam Shepard.** Byron and Ames are old friends, reunited by mutual desperation. Over bourbon on ice, they sit, reflect and bicker until fifty years of love, friendship and rivalry are put to the test at the barrel of a gun. "A poignant and honest continuation of themes that have always been present in the work of one of this country's most important dramatists, here reconsidered in the light and shadow of time passed." –NY Times. "Finely wrought…as enjoyable and enlightening as a night spent stargazing." –Talkin' Broadway. [2M] ISBN: 978-0-8222-2462-4

★ **ALL THE WAY by Robert Schenkkan. Winner of the 2014 Tony Award for Best Play.** November, 1963. An assassin's bullet catapults Lyndon Baines Johnson into the presidency. A Shakespearean figure of towering ambition and appetite, this charismatic, conflicted Texan hurls himself into the passage of the Civil Rights Act—a tinderbox issue emblematic of a divided America—even as he campaigns for re-election in his own right, and the recognition he so desperately wants. In Pulitzer Prize and Tony Award–winning Robert Schenkkan's vivid dramatization of LBJ's first year in office, means versus ends plays out on the precipice of modern America. ALL THE WAY is a searing, enthralling exploration of the morality of power. It's not personal, it's just politics. "…action-packed, thoroughly gripping… jaw-dropping political drama." –Variety. "A theatrical coup…nonstop action. The suspense of a first-class thriller." –NY1. [17M, 3W] ISBN: 978-0-8222-3181-3

★ **CHOIR BOY by Tarell Alvin McCraney.** The Charles R. Drew Prep School for Boys is dedicated to the creation of strong, ethical black men. Pharus wants nothing more than to take his rightful place as leader of the school's legendary gospel choir. Can he find his way inside the hallowed halls of this institution if he sings in his own key? "[An] affecting and honest portrait…of a gay youth tentatively beginning to find the courage to let the truth about himself become known." –NY Times. "In his stirring and stylishly told drama, Tarell Alvin McCraney cannily explores race and sexuality and the graces and gravity of history." –NY Daily News. [7M] ISBN: 978-0-8222-3116-5

★ **THE ELECTRIC BABY by Stefanie Zadravec.** When Helen causes a car accident that kills a young man, a group of fractured souls cross paths and connect around a mysterious dying baby who glows like the moon. Folk tales and folklore weave throughout this magical story of sad endings, strange beginnings and the unlikely people that get you from one place to the next. "The imperceptible magic that pervades human existence and the power of myth to assuage sorrow are invoked by the playwright as she entwines the lives of strangers in THE ELECTRIC BABY, a touching drama." –NY Times. "As dazzling as the dialogue is dreamful." –Pittsburgh City Paper. [3M, 3W] ISBN: 978-0-8222-3011-3

DRAMATISTS PLAY SERVICE, INC.
440 Park Avenue South, New York, NY 10016 212-683-8960 Fax 212-213-1539
postmaster@dramatists.com www.dramatists.com